ETF Investing Around the World

ETF Investing Around the World

A Guide to Building a Global ETF Portfolio

Carl T. Delfeld

President
Chartwell Partners
www.ChartwellETFadvisor.com

Followed by a Plan for America's Future:
"A Call to Economic Arms"

iUniverse, Inc.
New York Lincoln Shanghai

ETF Investing Around the World
A Guide to Building a Global ETF Portfolio

iUniverse books may be ordered through booksellers or by contacting:

iUniverse
2021 Pine Lake Road, Suite 100
Lincoln, NE 68512
www.iuniverse.com
1-800-Authors (1-800-288-4677)

ISBN-13: 978-0-595-42920-2 (pbk)
ISBN-13: 978-0-595-87258-9 (ebk)
ISBN-10: 0-595-42920-3 (pbk)
ISBN-10: 0-595-87258-1 (ebk)

Printed in the United States of America

Dedicated to Marilou, Jacqueline and Robert

Contents

Introduction
ETFs and a Global Perspective = Superior Returns

Exchange-traded funds, usually referred to as ETFs, have become the investment tool of choice by many investors and advisors. Now, whenever you see a list of investment choices, ETFs are right there besides stocks and mutual funds.

The advantages of ETFs have hit home with investors. They are easy to use, low cost, transparent, tax efficient, flexible and offer investors risk management options plus easy diversification. ETFs are exciting new investment tools that have grown rapidly to over $400 billion of assets and offer exposure to dozens of asset classes. 75% of all investment advisors use ETFs to some degree in building client portfolios.

ETFs are passively managed portfolios designed to track specific indexes and represent baskets of stocks, currencies or commodities. Some ETFs offer relatively low-risk, broadly diversified portfolios, which investors may find attractive as the core equity components of their portfolios.

In addition, the explosion of new and innovative ETFs over the past few years have given investors a wide variety of choice. There are now more than 450 ETFs on the market and more than a hundred in the pipeline.

It seems that every week a new ETF product is launched.

ChartwellETFadvisor.com has expanded along with the ETF market. I recognized the benefits of ETFs in 2002 while an investment advisor with UBS and at the end of that year formed the global investment advisory firm of Chartwell Partners and a newsletter and website dedicated to global ETF investing: ChartwellETFadvisor.com. Chartwell is also expanding its global ETF asset management through ETFArchitect.com and recently launched a blog for the global community of ETF investors at ETFXRAY.com..

We started with five ETF model portfolios: Core Conservative, Gone Fishing, International Opportunity, Global Opportunity, and Asian Opportunity. In 2006 we added a New Venture portfolio and for 2007 we added a Dividend/Income ETF portfolio.

But as valuable as ETFs are, they are still just an investment tool. Without a smart strategy and a clear risk management plan an investor can still run amok.

Our strategy is decidedly global. Without a global perspective, investors are missing a world of opportunity. While U.S. markets are still the largest, the rest of the world is catching up fast. The world is clearly filling in and the pace is accelerating due to tremendous breakthroughs in communication and technology.

*This Chartwell global edge was outlined in my first book "**Think Global, Grow Rich**" and the global theme amplified in my second book "**The New Global ETF Investor**" has helped build wealth for many Chartwell ETF members. Investors using a global approach and ETFs have certainly beat the U.S. only investors by taking advantage of growth and value opportunities around the world.*

During the past three years while the S&P 500 index was up 10%, the MSCI Emerging Market index ETF was up 26%, the MSCI Europe, Australia, Far East (EAFE) index ETF was up 20.7%, the Singapore and China ETFs, up 24%, the Sweden ETF, up 25% and the Australian ETF, up 23%.

In 2006, while S&P 500 investors earned a nice 14% return, the China ETF was up 84%, the Singapore ETF, up 46.7%, the Sweden ETF, up 43.4%, the Switzerland ETF, up 27.4%, the Malaysian, German and Austrian ETFs, up 37%, the Global Utilities ETF, up 38%, the Netherlands ETF, up 31% and the Hong Kong ETF was up 30% for the year. In early 2007, while U.S. markets were flat, the Singapore ETF was up 8.3% and the Malaysian ETF was already up 13.2%.

And the Chartwell Advisor's ETF portfolios have also done well. Below is a snapshot of returns.

	3-Year Average Annual Returns (2003-05)	2006
Core Conservative	+16.7%	+20.8%
Global	+27.2%	+24.7%
International	+29.8%	+27.3%
Asian	+26.2%	+21.9%
New Venture	NEW	+9.5%
Gone Fishing	+10.4%	+16.2%

The purpose of *"ETF Investing Around the World"* is to further explore ETF strategies and global opportunities. It is largely composed of a collection of articles I have published during the past year and is not meant to recommend specific ETFs. Please keep in mind that these articles do not necessarily represent what I would recommend to members at this time.

The articles will, however, be very helpful in learning about the different types of ETFs on the market and will also provide you with interesting intelligence on global stock markets such as Japan, Australia, Switzerland and emerging markets like India, China and Indonesia.

I hope you find these stories helpful and interesting and that you consider becoming a member of *www.ChartwellETFadvisor.com* or visiting my blog at *www.ETFXRAY.com*

Carl T. Delfeld
President
Chartwell Partners
ChartwellETFadvisor.com
Colorado Springs, CO

ETF Basics

The Case for ETFs

ETFs are exciting new investment tools that have grown rapidly to over $400 billion of assets. ETFs offer exposure to dozens of asset classes due to ETFs broad diversification, great flexibility, low expense ratios, high tax efficiency, competitive long-term performance versus active managers, and superior ETF trading flexibility.

ETFs are passively managed portfolios designed to track specific indexes and represent baskets of stocks, currencies or commodities. Some ETFs offer relatively low-risk, broadly diversified portfolios, which investors may find attractive as the core equity components of their portfolios. Others offer diversified investments in particular styles, sectors, industries, regions, countries, or commodities.

There are currently almost 300 ETFs that provide exposure to US equity markets. The largest ETF managers include Barclays Global Investors (iShares), State Street Global Advisors (streetTRACKs and SPDRs), Bank of New York (QQQQ), MDY, BLDRs), Vanguard, Merrill Lynch (HOLDRs), World Gold Trust, PowerShares, Rydex, ProShares, WisdomTree, DB Commodity Services, Victoria Bay, Van Eck, Claymore, First Trust, and Fidelity.

Several ETFs offer exposure to duplicate or similar indexes; however, there are significant differences in the products and indexes especially as to how they weight companies in the ETF basket. We believe investors should favor ETFs that best meet their investment objectives with the lowest operating expenses and reasonable liquidity.

There are 80 ETFs that provide international equity exposure. Many international ETFs are iShares based on MSCI Indexes, but others are based on S&P, Bank of New York ADR, Dow Jones STOXX, and WisdomTree indexes.

ETFs are an excellent tool to build a low cost and simple global portfolio. ETFs offer investors have many choices of global and international sector ETFs to allow them to take advantage of global growth and value opportunities around the world.

Six ETFs offer US fixed-income exposure. They are all iShares based on Lehman Treasury and Aggregate Indexes and a Goldman Sachs Corporate Bond Index. There are also ETFs that target dividend rich companies and preferred stock.

There are 14 ETFs that provide exposure to alternative asset classes including gold, silver, oil, broad based commodities and currencies. Three commodity ETFs hold the physical commodity in which they invest, while three other ETFs utilize commodity futures. The currency ETFs invest in foreign time deposits or currency futures.

ETFs trade on major exchanges. This allows investors to buy and sell them at stated market prices. In contrast to open-end funds that price once a day at the close, ETFs are available to all investors at market prices throughout the day. This helps to reduce the uncertainty of buying shares intraday at prices to be determined at the close. Many index-linked ETFs can also be shorted without an uptick, providing extra flexibility for hedging or market-timing.

ETFs are very flexible investment tools relative to mutual funds. They can be bought on margin, purchased using limit and stop loss orders, and many have listed options. This open trading prevents opportunities for market timing in which some investors buy open-end funds investing in foreign markets that closed before US trading started. For example, on a day when the US market is higher, ETFs based on a Japan index usually trade up in anticipation of higher prices in Japan overnight. In this case, open-end funds investing in Japan may be priced based on the previous day's close.

Index-linked ETFs have some of the lowest expenses of any investment tool. Their expense ratios are significantly lower than those of open-end mutual funds, but the range has widened as some providers cut fees while certain newer products have higher fees. For example, the Vanguard Total Stock Market Index Fund (VTI) has an expense ratio of seven basis points (bps), while the average actively managed domestic equity open-end fund has 150 bps in expenses.

ETFs are also tax efficient since the securities in the ETF basket only change as the index it tracks change. Mutual funds often distribute large amounts of capital gains to shareholders each year. ETFs capital gains distributions are rare and so ETF investors enjoy a lower tax burden which of course drags down returns.

For a complete list of ETFs, ETF sponsor information, articles about ETFs and performance data, please go to ETF Library.

ETF Portfolio Rules

Managing a global ETF portfolio does not have to be rocket science. Follow these eight steps and sleep easier.

1) **Liquidity First***: Before you even think of building an investment portfolio, you should set aside about six month of income in a "rainy day" account. This could be put into a money market fund or U.S. Treasury securities. Having this money set aside will ease your mind and allow you to be more open and creative with your global portfolios.*

2) **Separate Portfolios***: you should separate your core conservative portfolio from your growth portfolios. With the core conservative portfolio, your top priority is capital preservation and growth is a secondary consideration. Your growth portfolios are more speculative with capital growth as the primary goal.*

3) Really Diversify your Portfolios: You need positions in your portfolios that are likely to offset each other as unexpected events and market movements become a reality. This is not accomplished with different sectors ETFs or a mix of small cap, mid cap and large cap ETFs. Rather the goal is to have some investments that are on both sides of risks.

For example, if the US dollar declines, have some investments in precious metals or denominated in other currencies such as Switzerland or Australia or Singapore ETFs. If inflation heats up have some investments that hedge this risk such as timber, gold or Treasury inflation protected bonds (TIPs). If political events or policies in one country take a turn for the worst, it is helpful to have investments in other well developed countries to offset any loss of value.

You get the idea, spread your risk and avoid having one ETF account for more than 5-10% of your core portfolio.

4) Be Careful what Countries You Pick: You need some guidelines to help keep you from getting carried away and having too concentrated a position in a particular country or region.

In particular, take a good look at the following: 1) the stability and overall political and corporate governance, 2) the legal environment, respect for contracts, low levels of corruption, due process and rule of law, 3) the macroeconomic environment including fiscal discipline and currency strength, and 4) political risks that could affect financial markets.

Keep in mind that the quality of the countries you choose to invest in is the primary but not the only factor. The price or valuation of a country's stock market is also extremely important. Oftentimes the best time to buy into a country's stock market is when it is beaten down but there are signs that its economic and political problems will sharply improve. If you have a long-term perspective, you might consider annuities specially structured for ETF portfolios.

*5) **Minimize Company Risk** by using our "Buy Countries, Not Stocks" strategy that helps you minimize company risk. Instead of trying to pick the best three stocks on the Tokyo Stock Exchange, why not just minimize company risk by buying the Japan iShare ETF (EWJ) that tracks the Nikkei 225 and spread this risk amongst 225 Japanese companies. Or you could hedge your bets and do both.*

*6) **Monitor ETF Country and Company Exposure**: Be careful to look under the hood of ETFs to see where your money is going. For example, let's look at the iShares MSCI Emerging Markets ETF. It invests in 26 different countries so it is natural to think that you will get broad exposure to all 26 countries. You would be wrong: 50% of your investment in this fund is going to four countries: South Korea, South Africa, Taiwan and China. In addition, incredibly, 7.5% is going to one company, Samsung Electronics of South Korea.*

The same is true for the MSCI Europe, Asia and Far East (EAFE) index. It contains 21 developed countries but 48% of the money you invest would go to just two: Japan and the United Kingdom. Meanwhile less than 1% would go to Singapore and Ireland! Country specific ETFs such as the new China iShare (FXI) can also have a fair amount of concentrated risk. Although the China iShare tracks a basket of 25 companies, the largest 5 companies account for nearly 50% of your exposure.

*7) **Cut Losses with Trailing Stop Loss Policy and ETF Put Options**: We have all been there. You buy a stock or fund and it appreciates in value rapidly. Then it stumbles and begins to decline. What do you do? Should you buy more, let it ride, or sell?*

Save yourself a lot of pain and agony by following a simple rule. If a position ever falls more than 8% from its high, sell it immediately and reassess the situation. And if you invest in an ETF with a sizable downside risk, why not spend a few hundred dollars to purchase a put option as an insurance policy?

*8) **Rebalance Your Portfolio**: At least annually, you need to make some changes so that you are not overly exposed to countries that have higher risk factors and volatility. One way is by selling some shares of your winners and increasing exposure to under* *performers. This accomplishes another goal, locking in gains and taking some money off the table. Remember, only a fool holds out for top dollar especially in the more volatile emerging market countries.*

Building your portfolios with low-cost, tax-efficient ETFs is a smart strategy but don't set it on auto pilot.

Buy the Big Daddy of ETFs

While picking exchange-traded funds for you global portfolio, have you ever thought; "maybe I should invest in the companies that develop and sponsor the ETFs?" If so, now is the time to take a stake in Barclays PLC the sponsor iShares which is the largest family of ETFs.

Barclays PLC (BCS) is a huge global financial services firm with 114,000 employees and Barclays Bank is the flagship subsidiary that traces its roots back to the 17th century. It is the second largest bank in the UK servicing 14 million consumers and 600,000 businesses. This is a cash-cow business and the business bank profits have grown more than 20% annually since 2001. The bank is also active in France, Italy, Portugal and Spain as well in Asia and the Middle East.

A related business is Barclaycard which is Europe's biggest credit card issuer and accounts for about 13% of the groups total profits. Barclaycard issued the first credit card in the UK in 1966. Then there is the dynamic investment banking arm Barclays Capital which accounts for 23% of profits. This group focuses on debt and is getting stronger in Asia and emerging markets.

Now we come to the founder of iShares and second largest money manager in the world, Barclays Global Investors (BGI) that has operations in 47 countries and relationships with 2,500 clients. BGI created the first index strategy in 1971 and the first quantitative index strategy in 1978. Then came the creation of iShares in 2000 which ignited the ETF revolution in investing. I say revolution because iShares ETFs capitalized on and combined three major developments in 20th century investing: the growth in the popularity of common stocks, then mutual funds and finally indexing.

With more than 100 ETFs on the market iShares has garnered the majority of the ETF business and shows no signs of sitting on its lead. BGI now has more than $1.5 trillion under management and contributes 10% to Barclays bottom line while a sister group handling wealth management adds 3%. BGI now offers more than 111 *iShares ETFs totaling $207 billion assets under management. In May, 2005, it added ten new subsector ETFs.*

Just last week Morningstar raised its target price for Barclays PLC ADR (BCS) to $59, a nice premium to its current share price of $46 price. They estimate that the 20% return on equity for 2005 will rise to 24% and that operating profit will grow at an annual 12% clip through 2010.

Add the father of ETFs to complement your ETF portfolio.

The Powershares ETF Edge

While I tend to favor iShares an investment tool because of the wide menu and country specific options they provide investors, I have to say that I am increasingly impressed with the new and fast-growing Powershares family of ETFs and will be adding two of them to portfolios this month. Powershares also address one weakness of iShares which is that they track indexes that market cap weighted. In other words, the weighting of a company in a particular ETF is dependent on the value of its outstanding shares. This means that the bigger companies tend to affect the ETF's performance much more than the smaller companies. Of course, big doesn't always mean better. Powershares essentially creates its own indexes based on rules-based quantative analysis that they refer to as "intelligent indexes".

This seems to me to be more useful than blindly following market cap weighted indexes. There are two Powershares that I particularly like at this point. The first is a biotech Powershare (PBE) that contains 30 biotech companies. If its holdings were weighted by market cap, two companies, Amgen and Genentech would account for more than 60% of its holdings. Instead your exposure is spread among 30 different companies with no company accounting for more than 5% of the total. 30% of your exposure is to large cap companies, 26% is to mid-cap companies and 43% is to small cap companies. The biotech Powershare is an aggressive position so don't get carried away. I think it is a smart play on the tremendous opportunities for capital appreciation in the biotech industry which is showing some momentum after trading sideways since early 2004. The annual fee is only 0.60%.

The other Powershare that I like is the International Dividend Achievers Powershare which contains 42 ADRs traded on U.S. exchanges. I am usually not a big fan of ADRs since they usually trade at a premium to the underlying security but they do offer some comfort to investors since they meet U.S. reporting requirements and can be easily purchased on U.S. exchanges. The ADRs in this Powershare have to pass a stiff test: five fiscal years in a row of increased dividends.

Again the top holdings are no more than 5% of the total index and so you get great diversification. One problem with the most widely used international index, the MSCI Europe Asia & Far East Index (EAFE) is its concentration in Japan and the United Kingdom which account for almost 50% of the total index. Meanwhile exposure to promising countries such as Ireland and Hong Kong are less than 2%. Last year, the Powershares index beat the MSCI EAFE index by 7% and companies in the index averaged a 29% return on equity. The index is re-balanced quarterly and has an annual fee of 0.50%. Right now 67% of the companies in the index are large cap, 20% are mid-cap and 13% are small cap companies.

300 Million People, 300 ETFs

As the American population crossed the 300 million mark, the number of ETFs on the market passed 300. No doubt many investors are a bit confused as to how they differ and which ones they should pick for their portfolios.

When the rubber hits the road, there are two ETF issues that are paramount: what companies are in the ETF basket and how are they weighted in the basket. A less than perfect analogy would be a trip to the grocery store. With a mutual fund, immediately upon entering you hand over your grocery cart to a fund manager and they wander through the store picking items for you. With an ETF, you hand it over to a robot that goes down the aisles selecting items based on some process such as shelf space, nutrition or food group. Value investors might only buy items on sale.

About 90% of the ETFs out there weight the companies in the basket based on their market capitalization or market value. This is the number of shares outstanding times the current share price. Market value weighting of companies in indexes is the conventional norm and widely accepted by the institutional establishment.

The largest family of ETFs on the market is iShares and all their ETFs are market cap weighted. There is almost no chance that they will deviate from this philosophy. Recognizing the tremendous lead that iShares ETFs has built, their competitors have little choice but to innovate with other strategies to capture market share.

For example, Rydex launched in 2003 the S&P equal weight ETF (RSP) which weighs each of the companies in the S&P 500 index equally at 2% each rather than the top heavy market cap weighted index. When the big stocks soar such as in the late

1990s, RSP will lag but in the difficult 2000-2005 period, the annualized return for the equal weight ETF was 8.06% versus 1.13% for the traditional index. This week Rydex is introducing nine new U.S. sector equal weighted ETFs which represent the different sectors that make up the S&P 500 index. The new sector ETFs will cover consumer discretionary, consumer staples, energy, financial services, healthcare, industrial, basic materials, technology and utilities.

The Powershares ETFs take another approach. They create an index and weight companies in the ETF basket based on a model which they describe but do not disclose. Normally, they have a maximum weighting policy which prevents large companies from dominating the basket. The weightings of companies in the Powershares ETF baskets fall between the extremes of the market value and equal weight. One issue is that investors won't know for some time whether the models will yield superior returns.

Another fairly new approach is that offered by the Wisdom Tree family of ETFs. Wisdom Tree weights companies in their ETF baskets by their record of increasing cash dividends. This gives investors another pattern of distribution and falls between the extremes. Backtesting shows a performance advantage over market cap weighting but time will tell. Wisdom Tree recently introduced 11 international sector ETFs and offers unique ETFs in areas such as international small cap and mid cap ETFs.

Don't become overwhelmed by the choices out there. The Chartwell ETF Advisor uses a blend of these different ETFs in building its model ETF portfolios for members. Each family of ETFs offers a philosophy that will work best in different markets. We sold the S&P 500 equal weight ETF some time ago and moved into a market cap weighted one to take advantage of the rotation to mega cap. Think of your ETF portfolio as a cooking recipe, the ingredients need to blend well together and do not stand alone.

Don't forget to "look under the hood" of an ETF before buying it. You certainly don't buy things in the grocery store without even looking at them.

ETF Innovations Continue

Even as ETFs have gone main stream, the innovations continue. Here is a review of some new creative ETFs that have been launched or will shortly hit the market.

First Trust Advisors now has eight ETFs available to investors. The First Trust NASDAQ-100 Equal Weighted ETF (QQEWI) weights each of the 100 non-financial companies in the index equally and then rebalances on a quarterly basis. This avoids the problem in the market-cap weighted QQQQ where the ten largest companies in the index account for 40% of the total value. Another good option that does not get the attention it deserves is the Fidelity ETF, (ONEQ), which tracks the NASDAQ composite index of 3,000 companies. It too is market cap weighted but has somewhat better balance since the top ten holdings represent 29% of the basket's value.

The First Trust IPOX-100 ETF (FPX) is a basket that includes the 100 largest, most liquid initial public offerings ("IPOs") in the U.S. IPOX Composite Index. No one IPO can account for more that 10% of the ETF and the index it tracks measures the average performance of U.S. IPOs during the first 1,000 trading days.

Pro Fund Advisors is launching this week its first eight ETFs that allow investors to go long and short popular indexes in a cost effective manner. The ETFs will track the Nasdaq 100, the S&P 500, the Dow Jones Industrial Average (DJIA) and the S&P Midcap 400.

The ETFs that will target 200% of the value of the underlying indexes are Nasdaq 100 (QLD), S&P 500 (SSO), DJIA (DDM) and S&P Midcap 400 (MVV).

The Pro Fund ETFs that will target 100% of the inverse performance of the underlying indexes are the Nasdaq 100 (PSQ), S&P 500 (SH), DJIA (DOG) and S&P Midcap 400 (MYY). The expense ratio for these new ETFs will be 0.95%.

Rydex is launching six additional currency ETFs to build on the popular Euro ETF (FXE) as a hedge on the U.S. dollar. The currency ETFs will benchmark to the spot price versus the $USD and the strategy for each is to return the spot price, plus interest, less the trust expenses. These new products may be available to investors in about a week and will trade under the following tickers: British Pound (FXB), Canadian Dollar (FXC), Mexican Peso (FXM), Australian Dollar (FXA), Swiss Franc (FXF) and the Swedish Krona (FXS).

The largest family of ETFs, iShares, is not resting on its laurels but continues to press ahead with new ETFs. Its ten iShares Dow Jones U.S. Subsector ETFs, launched on May 1st, gives investors the ability to slice the sector markets thinly. Some examples are the Broker-Dealer iShare (IAI), the Insurance iShare (IAK), the Oil Equipment & Services iShare (IEO), the Aerospace & Defense iShare (ITA) and the Regional Banks iShare (IAT). All are market cap weighted with an expense ratio of 0.48%. The Regional Banks iShare has a decent dividend yield of 3.21%.

Some of the indexes that these new ETFs track have done quite well over the last three years through March of this year. The Oil Exploration & Production index was up

49%, the Aerospace & Defense index was up 38.3% and the Investment Services index was up 49.7%.

But if you like me prefer equal-weighted ETFs and want sector and industrial ETF exposure, State Street Global Advisors has exactly what you need with this Thursday's launch of six new ETFs. Based on S&P Total Market Select Industry Indexes, they are (XME) Metals & Mining, (XRE) Retail, (XPH) Pharma, (XES) Oil & Gas Equipment & Services, (XOP) Oil & Gas Exploration & Production, and (KRE) Regional Banks which is a equal-weighted basket of 50 US regional bank stocks.

iShares has also recently introduced its iPath Dow Jones-AIG Commodity Index Total Return Exchange-Traded Notes. This is a mouthful but essentially this ETF are unsecured debt securities issued by Barclays Bank PLC that are linked to the total returns of the index .

This iShares commodity ETF (DJP) has an expense fee of 0.75% and provides exposure to the following commodity groups: energy 30%, livestock 9%, precious metals 9%, industrial metals 21% and agriculture 31%. Based on monthly returns from March 1991 through March of this year, the index has had only a correlation of 9% to the S&P 500 index and 23% to the MSCI EAFE index. The index is currently is made up of the prices of 19 exchange traded futures contracts.

Chartwell members seem to be looking for more international products such as country-specifics for more emerging market countries and some fixed income international ETFs. I have been working on a equal-weighted EAFE index which an ETF could track easily. The market cap-weighted EAFE iShare (EFA) has 49% allocated to Japan and the UK and my numbers show that an equal-weighted EAFE has outperformed the market cap weighted index by a substantial margin over a three, five and ten year period.

This explosion in choice over the past few years is a blessing and a challenge. Choose carefully and get some good advice from an ETF specialist.

ETF Tax Planning

While exchange-traded funds (ETFs) are well known for their low cost, transparency and flexibility, the tax efficiency advantage of ETFs oftentimes gets overlooked. As we head into the last month of the year, let's look at how investors may lower their tax liabilities by converting some positions in their portfolio to ETFs as well as discuss other

ETF strategies to reduce tax burdens. Since every investment situation is different, please be sure to consult tax counsel before taking action.

Like higher expenses, tax consequences can negatively impact fund performance. ETFs are more tax efficient than actively managed mutual funds. Some mutual fund managers are prone to selling position late in the year to lock in capital gains. These gains are then distributed to current shareholders on a pro rata basis.
Because ETFs track indexes which generally buy and sell securities far less often than mutual funds, most ETFs rarely distribute any pesky end-of-the-year capital gains distributions that are detailed in those 1099 forms that collect in your tax file. iShares, the largest family of ETFs, has never distributed any capital gains to iShares investors.

In addition, mutual fund shareholders purchase and redeem shares from the fund—which may result in gains distributed to all shareholders. The killer is that these capital gains known in the investment business as "imbedded capital gains" may come from the sale of a mutual fund stock holding that goes back many years—well before the current shareholder invested in the fund. In contrast to mutual fund investors, ETF shareholders buy and sell ETFs on an exchange, a transaction that does not affect other shareholders. ETF investors clearly have better control and transparency of their tax situation.

While you can see the tax advantages of ETFs, you may not be aware of their use as a toll to reduce your tax burden. Let me highlight a few of them.

Let's assume you have a small cap mutual fund that has declined $15,000 since its purchase three years ago and you want to apply the capital loss but still want small cap exposure. You could sell the mutual fund and simultaneously invest the proceeds in the iShares Russell 2000 ETF (IWM). The key is to avoid switching to an ETF that is similar but not identical or you may come into conflict of the wash sale rule whereby buying the same or a substantially identical security within 30 days after a sale defers the capital loss. You could then apply this $15,000 towards other capital gains distributions to lower your overall tax liabilities.

You could also use this tax loss harvesting to re-balance your overall portfolio. In the above example, you might have wanted to cut back a bit on small cap exposure and allocated more to a large cap ETF like the Vanguard Large Cap ETF.

An investor could also use ETFs to take care of a collection of individual stocks which are being held at a loss. For example, an investor with a loss on a portfolio of healthcare stocks could sell the securities and then purchase a sector ETF such as the iShares Dow Jones U.S. Healthcare Sector ETF (IYH).

Switching from a loss position in an actively managed mutual fund to an ETF of course has double barreled tax benefits. First you can take the capital loss without losing the exposure, and secondly, you have a more tax efficient position with a much lower likelihood of future capital gains distributions.

Take some time this month to review your portfolios with your investment or tax advisor. It is a great time to consider expanding your ETF holdings with the bonus of perhaps lowering overall tax liabilities for both this year and for future years.

Filling in the World with ETFs

While my focus right now is on overseas markets, America remains a very attractive country in which to invest in.

700 of world's largest 2,000 companies are headquartered in U.S. and America has the world's deepest and broadest capital markets. America is No doubt the fastest growing economy of the large industrialized countries and has created a net 30 million new jobs over the last 20 years. During the same period, Europe has created zero net new jobs.

Our economy is flexible, dynamic and open. Looking for proof? 75% of America's top 100 firms did not even exist in 1980

But, even if you agree with me that, despite its problems, the U.S. is the greatest country in the history of world—I cannot advocate strongly enough the need for you to have a global perspective in building your portfolios.

I say this because the world is filling in and developing countries are rapidly catching up. Let's keep in mind that 200 years ago, when this country was just getting started, China was the world's largest economy. 50 years ago, the U.S. accounted for 50% of world GDP—now it is closer to 20%. By the way, this is still a very impressive number.

Europe was devastated by WWII and China and India (40% of humanity) took a wrong turn to follow the Soviet style command model becoming frozen in socialism and communism. In the 1980's, both finally began to open up to the world and pursue market reforms

And, there is no doubt that breakthroughs in communications and technology are accelerating how quickly countries are catching up—what used to take decades now can take only a few years

For example, there are 9 trillion emails and sent each day more than a billion google searches done each day and there are now 2 billion cell phones are now in global circulation.

To underscore and highlight the dramatic changes taking place in global economy, here are some snapshots of global trends and the related ETF investment opportunities.

China (FXI) now has world's largest FX reserves—$1 trillion. India (IIF) is adding 25 MM citizens (the size of Canada's entire population) to the ranks of middle class each year. The U.S. has not been the world's best stock market in 16 years. Japan's (EWJ) bilateral trade with China is now greater than its trade with America. According to KPMG the least expensive places in the world to conduct business are Canada (EWC) and Singapore (EWS).

The Brazil (EWZ) stock market is up over 100% last 12 months. The country is now energy sufficient due to use of sugarcane for ethanol production. Taiwan (EWT) and South Korea (EWY) now export more to China than to the U.S. 25% of world's population 25 years and younger live in India (IIF). According to Barclays Capital, Asia has received $670 billion of net capital inflows since 2001.

Europe is still sitting on 40% of the world's wealth and even though its economy is flat, Germany's ETF (EWG) is up 42% during the last year. While GM debt relegated to junk bond status,—80% of market value of global auto makers accounted by Nissan, Toyota (TM) and Honda (HMC).

So keep the U.S. at the core of your global portfolio but open it up to overseas opportunities using low-cost and tax-efficient ETFs as your core investment tool.

ETF Shock Absorbers

The coordinated interest rate increase by the European Central Bank (ECB) and the UK by 0.25% last Friday increases the likelihood that the Fed will follow suit on Tuesday. The UK benchmark rate is now 5.45%, the ECB is 3%, the U.S. is 5.25% and Australia is at 6%.

Most analysts expecting another Fed rate hike point to continued inflationary pressures particularly in the energy sector. I think that a more important consideration is the need for higher rates to defend or more aptly manage the decline of the U.S. dollar.

Either way, markets will likely react unfavorably.

The escalation of tensions in the Middle East, fireworks courtesy of North Korea, 50% of the world's natural gas reserves in the hands of Russia and Iran, pressure on the U.S. dollar and the random exogenous events that impact markets can keep the most optimistic global investor like me awake at night.

How can an investor mitigate the risk that such events will derail their well thought out portfolio? Having sizable cash positions helps. Diversification into commodities, precious metals, fixed income, hard currencies, energy, safe haven countries like Switzerland may also blunt the blow of volatile global equity markets.

But there is another tool that can act as a "shock absorber" for your portfolio. There are now ETFs that whose value moves inversely to changes in specific indexes like the S&P 500 (SH), Dow Jones Industrial Average (DOG), NASDAQ 100 (PSQ) and the S&P Midcap (MYY) indexes. With a few clicks of your mouse you can transform your portfolio into a long-short fund, not a bad idea in a market that at best lacks direction.

How much of a shock absorber your portfolio should have depends on your personal financial situation. I have a 10% position in our core portfolio.

Which inverse moving ETFs should you pick? The S&P 500 is a good broad choice and the NASDAQ 100 has worked well for me this year.

I wish there was an ETF that moved inversely to a small cap index. While small caps have outperformed larger cap indexes for the last seven years, my hunch is that the cycle is turning. In July the Russell 2000 was down 4.7%, the Russell 1000 was flat and the mega 50 index of the largest 50 companies was up 2.3%. The flight to quality, size and liquidity seems natural to me with increasing geopolitical uncertainty and at this stage of the business cycle. At the very least, you should pull back on small cap allocations.

Having an allocation to some inverse moving ETFs will be a drag on your portfolio performance if markets uniformly rise but it is nice to see some black on your portfolio screen stand out on days when others see only a sea of red numbers.

Rifle and Shotgun ETFs

Many financial advisors advocate the lower cost broad-based international ETFs over country ETFs but you can easily shoot yourself in the foot by being penny wise and pound foolish.

A common question I get at ETF conferences and workshops is whether investors should use broad-based international ETFs or country-specific ETFs to play international growth?

The answer is, of course, it depends on what type of investor you are. What is your risk profile, your return objectives and what is the pattern of distribution in the ETF basket under consideration? I often use the analogy of a rifle and shotgun. You don't go turkey hunting with a rifle and it would be foolhardy to try to nail that trophy bighorn with a shotgun.

In general, if you are a long-term buy and hold investor, then perhaps a broad ETF will get the job done. But don't get all tangled up in the bush by basing your decision on the lowest cost ETF Study the options before making your choice.

The most popular broad international ETF on the market is the one that tracks the MSCI Europe, Australia and Far East Index also known as the EAFE. This index contains 21 well developed countries and one ETF that tracks it is the iShares (EFA) with an annual expense ratio of 0.35%.

Sounds good but the problem is that because the country stock markets are weighted in the index and ETF by the value of the markets. 50% of your money will go to two countries: Japan and the United Kingdom. Meanwhile only 1% of your money will go to dynamic countries with great stock markets like Ireland. The Singapore weighting in this basket is 0.77%, Austria is 0.58%, Hong Kong is 1.75%, and Sweden is 2.46%.

Not a good move especially this year with the Japan ETF flat as a pancake and Singapore (EWS) up 32%, Hong Kong (EWH) up 19.5%, Sweden (EWD) up 32% and Austria (EWO) up 23%. These country-specific ETF bullets will cost you a slightly higher annual fee but the added flexibility is well worth the cost.

The Vanguard Pacific ETF (VPL) is another example of an ETF that absolutely requires looking under the hood. It looks like a shotgun but is actually a rifle. Investors may think they are getting broad exposure to the Pacific region but 74% of the money in this ETF basket goes to Japan with an additional 17% to Australia. With an annual fee of just 0.18% bargain hunters might have been smiling when they bought it and I have to admit that it does have 20% of its net assets in some great companies like Toyota, BHP and Honda.

Still, it is an awfully big bet on Japan and if you are looking to tap into robust Asia-Pacific growth, keep this ETF in your holster and fire away with the China iShare

(FXI) up 46% so far this year, Singapore (EWS), up 32%, Malaysia (EWM) up 22.5%, Australia (EWA) up 22% not to mention more dicey markets like Indonesia which is up 58% this year.

In emerging markets of course putting too much powder behind one country can blow up in your face. This is why ETFs that track the MSCI Emerging Markets index may be the best strategy for many investors. The iShares Emerging Market ETF (EEM) gives you a nice balance with roughly 16% exposure to South Korea, 11% to Taiwan, 10% to Brazil, 10% to China, 10% to Russia and 9% to South Africa. The Vanguard Emerging Market ETF (VWO) has similar country weightings but has an annual fee of only 0.30% compared to 0.75% for the iShares (EFA) ETF.

There are also other options out there such as the new eleven Wisdom Tree international sector ETFs and the global sector ETFs which normally have about half of their baskets in foreign stocks. Depending on the stakes, you might also consider getting a guide to increase the likelihood of bagging your game. After all, it wouldn't be smart to go hunting in foreign territory without taking someone along that knows the terrain.

ETFs Unplugged

Exchange-traded funds (ETFs) are great investment tools but most have a flaw that investors and advisors usually miss. Let's take a look under the hood and introduce some new and innovative ETF products.

Essentially, ETFs are nothing more than an index fund that trades like a stock. Because of their simplicity, flexibility, low cost and tax efficiency they are growing fast. Last year the Barclays iShares family of ETFs brought in more new money than the Fidelity mutual fund machine.

Unfortunately, many investors and advisors are building portfolios of ETFs without looking inside the box and seeing where the money is going. One of the chief goals of a portfolio is diversification and many ETFs are not very diversified. This is because the companies in the ETF are weighted by size—specifically by the market value of its outstanding stock. This can result in an unwise concentration of risk and uneven performance.

The index fund community's preoccupation with market cap weighting may have a strong theoretical basis but to me it is contrary to common sense. To be blunt, I pay very little attention to it while building global portfolios for clients.

Most investors would agree that just because a company is bigger doesn't mean that it is a better investment. Let's look at the most well known index—the S&P 500 index. Many investors think that investing in the S&P 500 means that their money is being divided equally between 500 companies. This is far from the truth. Because the companies are weighted by size, 22% of your investment is going to the ten largest companies in the index and 60% of your investment is going to the largest 50 companies in the index.

This is why I have been advising clients to invest in the Rydex S&P 500 equal-weight ETF (RSP) which weights each company in the index equally. In 2003 the equal weight S&P 500 ETF beat the S&P index by 11%, in 2004 it beat the index by 5% and year-to-date it is up slightly while the S&P index is down.

In my book, "The New Global Advisor", I ask readers a provocative question. If you wanted exposure to the dynamic biotechnology industry, would you prefer to primarily invest in a few large well know biotech companies or would you prefer to spread your investment over thirty biotech companies? If you're the former, you might invest in the iShares Nasdaq Biotechnology ETF (IBB) whereby 25% of your investment would go to three companies. For those that prefer broader exposure including some small cap companies, I have discovered a new family of ETFs called Powershares.

The new and innovative Powershares family of ETFs essentially creates its own indexes based on rules-based quantitative analysis that they refer to as "intelligent indexes". This seems to me to be more useful than blindly following market cap weighted indexes. There are two Powershares that I particularly like at this point. The first is the biotech Powershare (PBE) that contains 30 biotech companies. If its holdings were weighted by market cap, two companies would account for more than 60% of its holdings. Instead your exposure is spread among 30 different companies with no company accounting for more than 5% of the total. 30% of your exposure is to large cap companies, 26% is to mid-cap companies and 43% is to small cap companies.

The biotech Powershare is an aggressive position so don't get carried away. I think it is a smart play on the tremendous opportunities for capital appreciation in the biotech industry which is showing some momentum after trading sideways since early 2004. The annual fee is only 0.60%.

The other Powershare that I like is the International Dividend Achievers Powershare (PID) that contains 42 ADRs traded on U.S. exchanges. I am usually not a big fan of ADRs since they usually trade at a premium to the underlying security but they do offer some comfort to investors since they meet U.S. reporting requirements and can be *easily purchased on U.S. exchanges. The ADRs in this Powershare have to pass a stiff test: five fiscal years in a row of increased dividends. Again the top holdings are no more than 5% of the total index and so you get great diversification.*

One problem with the most widely used international index, the MSCI Europe, Asia & Far East Index (EAFE) is its concentration in Japan and the United Kingdom which account for almost 50% of the index's total value. Meanwhile exposure to promising countries such as Ireland and Hong Kong are less than 2%.

Last year, this Powershares index beat the MSCI EAFE index by 7% and companies in the ETF averaged a 29% return on equity. The index is re-balanced quarterly and has an annual fee of 0.50%. Right now 67% of the companies in the index are large cap, 20% are mid-cap and 13% are small cap companies.

Getting the right blend of ETFs takes some time and effort. Remember that all ETFs are not equal and choose carefully.

Better than Diamonds

What is still the most-quoted market indicator in newspapers, on TV and on the Internet—the Dow Jones Industrial Index (DJIA) which has recently made it past its January 2000 high.

Let's look briefly at the history of this index, and through the use of our ETF XRAY highlight why it may be out of date and discuss some better ETF options than the Dow Diamonds (DIA) to tap into the mega-cap trend.

Charles Dow created in 1896 the first Dow Jones Index that included nine railroad stocks, a steamship line and a communications company. In 1916, the industrial average expanded to 20 stocks; the number was raised again, in 1928, to 30, where it remains.

Today, the DJIA is a benchmark that tracks American stocks that are considered to be the leaders of the economy and are listed on the Nasdaq and NYSE. The DJIA covers 30 large-cap companies, which are subjectively picked by the editors of the Wall Street Journal. Over the years, companies in the index have been changed to ensure the index stays current in its measure of the U.S. economy. In fact, of the initial companies included, only General Electric remains as part of the modern-day average.

The most recent deletions were when Kodak, International Paper, and AT&T were replaced by Pfizer, AIG, and Verizon. A few years ago, the Dow's overseers made history by adding the first two stocks listed not on the New York Stock Exchange, but on the Nasdaq: Microsoft and Intel. Since 1959, other companies added include Disney, Wal-Mart, McDonald's, and Home Depot.

You may be thinking that the S&P 500 Index has overtaken the DJIA in popularity. But over long stretches, the Dow 30 and the S&P 500 have correlated closely. The S&P 500 Index is also market-cap weighted leading to an unhealthy concentration in the largest stocks. This index is 12% off its 2000 peak.

As the Dow Average breaks 2000 highs it is important to note that only ten of the thirty companies have actually accomplished this feat. Since January 2000, Altria is up 200%, Caterpillar about 150% followed by companies like Boeing and Exxon-Mobil. Twenty companies such as JP Morgan Chase, HP, IBM, Intel and Disney are still below 2000 levels. In addition, if we adjust the Dow Average for inflation, its real peak is 14,100.

I suggest that investors might be better off trading their Diamonds for the Rydex Mega 50 ETF (XLG) which tracks an index of the largest fifty U.S. stocks. Another good pick would be (SDY) whose basket includes the 50 highest yielding stocks in the S&P 1500. If you think the Dow is overbought you might consider the new Pro Funds ETF that moves inversely to the Dow and trades under the apt symbol (DOG).

Because the DJIA is made up of exclusively U.S. companies and by definition focused on industrial companies, it does not accurately reflect the performance of large swaths of the U.S. or global marketplace. There are a lot of good companies in the DJIA but it is no longer a good barometer of the American economy or the typical American portfolio nor a useful index for investment vehicles to track.

For example, since the trough in early 2003, the Dow is up 56% while the broadest measure on international stocks, the Dow Jones Wilshire Global Index is up 137% and countries like Japan and Germany are up over 100%. A great play for a global investor is the S&P Global 100 ETF (IOO) that includes exposure to 100 of the largest companies in the world. About 50% are American companies. Year to date, it is up 13% and has decisively beaten the Dow and the Diamonds.

The Dow Jones Industrial Average was revolutionary at inception and has a well deserved storied past that parallels the evolution of the American economy. For the era of the global economy and investor, it's time for a new revolution. ETFs are the core investment tool of the future and ETF XRAY will help you look under the hood to make wise choices.

With many Asian stock markets having a great year, it is unlikely that many investors are thinking much these days about dividends. This is unfortunate given their importance to total returns over the long haul and their value to buffer portfolios in down markets.

It used to be that the primary reason investors purchased shares was for their dividend stream. But now the role of dividends relative to total returns is under appreciated by most investors even though companies in the Asia-Pacific region offer some of the highest payout ratios in the world. If you look at the last twenty years, the re-investment of dividends accounted for more than 50% of total market returns for the MSCI All Country Asia-Pacific Index.

These dividends can be likened to low hanging fruit on a tree. The tree's growth represents capital appreciation but its fruit can be periodically plucked just like dividends are regularly distributed into investor's portfolio baskets.

In a down market, dividends also act as a "shock absorber" softening the blow from declining share prices. Dividends can also serve a useful signal for investors. A cut in dividends might highlight a company's cash flow problem or unexpected expenses. A record of increasing dividends could signal a more optimistic profit picture and a stronger financial health. The expectation by investors of steady dividends also disciplines management and forces them to make careful capital allocation decisions. Finally, I like dividends because all shareholders are treated equally. Small investors get the same proportion of dividends as a shareholder holding a controlling interest in a company.

As of the end of 2005, the dividends paid by companies in Asia have varied by country quite significantly. New Zealand companies lead the list with a dividend yield of 4.8%. Thailand is at 4.3%, Australia at 3.6% and Singapore at 3.4%. Australia's tax system generally avoids double taxation for domestic investors which probably encourages its companies to distribute a healthy share of profits to shareholders.

Japanese companies are not known for high dividend payouts and therefore it is not surprising that their companies are at the bottom with 0.9% dividend yield. This may be changing however as companies become more responsive to shareholder activism and as the potential of many Japanese companies to pay higher dividends has increased commensurately with their rising profits as the Japanese economy tentatively recovers from its long slump.

Another measure of dividends is the percentage of net profits distributed to shareholders as dividends. This is known as the dividend payout ratio. New Zealand leads with a payout ratio of 66%, followed by Taiwan with 59%, Singapore with 48% and Australia with 45%. Japan is a laggard with 21% and South Korea is at the bottom of the list with a 20% dividend payout ratio. This is one reason that South Korea's stock market valuations usually lag other stock markets in the region.

If you want to add more on high dividend companies in your global portfolios, there are several ways to approach it.

Screening individual companies by their dividend yields is one option. China Mobile has an attractive 3.8% dividend yield although its share price has taken a hit recently as investors sold ahead of a Hang Seng index reshuffle that could dilute the stock's weighting. Melbourne-based National Australia Bank has a nice 4.3% dividend yield with a return on equity of 15.7% and trades at 2.2 times book value.

Wisdom Tree exchange-traded funds (ETFs) are also an excellent tool since they weight companies in their ETF baskets by company's record of paying cash dividends. Investors thus capture this dividend stream and also gain a sell discipline since company weightings are rebalanced based on annualized quarterly dividends. When Ford (F) recently slashed its dividend, it was cut from some Wisdom Tree ETFs.

Some choices are Wisdom Tree's Pacific ex-Japan Total Dividend ETF (DND) which has quite a few Australian companies and for Japan the High Yielding Japan Equity ETF (DNL). And while small cap companies are usually not associated with big dividends, this is not always the case so check out Wisdom Tree's International Small Cap Dividend ETF (DLS).

Lastly, Asian specialist Matthews Funds recently introduced an Asia Pacific Equity Income no-load mutual fund (MAPIX). The fund's objective is total return with an emphasis on generating current income by investing in high dividend companies.

Keep a healthy dose of dividend rich companies in your portfolio to top off returns in strong markets and cushion the pain when share prices decline.

Global ETF Strategies

Pick Countries, Not Stocks

You can build an ETF portfolio that beats international index benchmarks and mutual funds because of the flexibility and advantages ETFs offer you over both.

Let's start with looking at how the widely used MSCI Europe, Asia, Australia and Far East (EAFE) index is put together. The EAFE index contains 21 countries and, like all the MSCI indexes, it weights countries based on the size of their stock markets. This leads to 49% of the EAFE allocated to only two countries: Japan and the UK. Add in France and Germany and the percentage climbs over 65%. Meanwhile, the allocation to more dynamic countries such as Ireland and Austria is 0.82% and 0.54%, respectively.

This bias towards size presents independent investors with a great opportunity to beat the index funds and benchmarks. How? By ignoring country weightings in the indexes and independently selecting and weighting countries in their portfolio based on their valuations, fiscal discipline, growth potential, capital flows, currencies, and pace of market reforms.

An excellent investment tool to implement this strategy of challenging the index country weightings is the 22 country-specific ETFs created by iShares. These ETFs track a leading index in a specific country. For example, the Japan iShare (EWJ) tracks the Nikkei 225 index. The country iShares allow you to buy into markets from Singapore (EWS) to Switzerland (EWL) with a click of your mouse.

What about the risk of investing in smaller stock markets? It seems to me that investing in a vehicle tracking the MSCI EAFE index with 49% exposure to Japan and the UK is riskier than investing 10% of your portfolio in each of ten countries such as Canada, Singapore, Australia, Ireland, Switzerland and Hong Kong.

Now, let's turn to some of the advantages your international ETF portfolio will have over actively managed mutual funds.

First, in my experience covering international equity managers, most will hug the index country weightings or only deviate from them on the margins. Therefore, they will tend to have the same big market bias of the indexes.

Second, ETFs are lower-cost and more tax efficient, transparent, and flexible than mutual funds. While the annual expense ratio and 12b-1 fees for the Templeton Foreign Fund are 1.4%, country iShare annual fees range from 0.50% to 0.74%. Rock bottom discount brokerage fees make the cost of trading ETFs almost a non-issue. More importantly, iShares have not distributed any capital gains during the past four years.

ETFs trade like a stock so you can buy and sell them throughout the trading day. You can also put in place risk management tools like trailing stop loss orders or options. In addition, ETFs are transparent and investors can at any time see exactly what is in the basket of securities that make up an ETF. Another benefit of investing overseas ETFs is that they are not hedged against the dollar. For example, if the U.S. dollar falls relative to the Swiss Franc, the returns to Americans investing in the Swiss iShare will be higher in dollar terms.

Despite these ETF advantages, you will still need a global strategy to help you pick and weight country ETFs in your portfolio.

For example, your portfolio might include the Austrian iShare (EWO) as an excellent play on low-cost Eastern European markets. Singapore (EWS) and Hong Kong (EWH) are great ways to play China's economic growth. Australia (EWA) represents a well developed and diversified economy at the heart of Asia-Pacific growth and on the sweet spot of commodities. Switzerland (EWL) is a safe haven in times of instability and Canada (EWC) has a significant exposure to the energy sector.

To tap into the high growth rates of emerging markets include some exposure to countries such as Brazil (EWZ), Malaysia (EWM), and Taiwan (EWT). For countries that do not yet have an ETF, consider using closed-end funds like the Morgan Stanley India Fund (IIF), the Indonesia Fund (IF) and the Thai Fund (TF) as proxies. Weight these markets in your portfolio like spices, a little is tasty but too much can be dangerous.

Don't forget to look "under the hood" of ETFs to see what securities are in the basket. There can be a heavy concentration in just a few stocks. And if you would rather not manage your international ETF portfolio, consider using an investment advisor that specializes in international portfolios and ETFs. Newport Beach based Global Trends Investments is one ETF advisor that has both a global perspective and a disciplined 8% stop loss strategy.

So if you want your international portfolio to outperform index benchmarks and mutual funds, I suggest that you unshackle yourself from the country weightings and build a creative blend of country-specific ETFs.

Emerging Market ETFs: What's Next?

Exchange-Traded Funds (ETFs) tracking emerging markets have had a remarkable run. In 2005, the South Korea (EWY) was been up 57%, Brazil (EWZ) up 56%, Mexico (EWW) up 49% and the Emerging Markets (EEM) up 34%. In the last 12 months, China (FXI) has shown some life up 26% and South Africa is up 32%.

The MSCI Emerging Market index is up 82% since mid-2004. In addition, lower risk countries like Singapore (EWS) have been up for four straight years and its Straits Times Index has risen by 85% since 2003.

I am getting a lot of call lately about what to do next. Should investors buy, hold or sell?

There are two arguments out there about the future of emerging markets at polar extremes from each other. BCA Research notes that despite the run up in prices over the past three years, trailing and forward PEs are only 13 and 11 respectively. Both are far from being out of line from both a fundamental and a historical basis. Brazil is a good example with a market at about 10 times earnings.

Morgan Stanley took a different view in a research report published last week. It points to the shrinking of the sovereign risk premium for emerging markets as a sign of potential weakness. In other words, the degree of higher interest rates demanded from the market to offset the higher risk of emerging markets has shrunk sharply. In 2004 it was 3.5% and now it is about 0.50%. There can be little doubt that this shrinkage has fueled at least part of the rise in emerging markets.

The truth probably lies in the middle of these extremes. The world is filling in and emerging markets will very likely outperform more mature markets but don't expect a straight line up. Near term there will be some pullbacks in specific countries depending on circumstances.

Be alert, get some good intelligence, and put in place some measures to control risk. Here are a few ideas.

First, follow our portfolio approach whereby we weigh each ETF in a portfolio to prevent getting carried away with too large a position in an emerging market ETF. It is a bit like dining out, you may like Thai food once in a while but do you want it every night?

Second, keep emerging market ETFs out of your core portfolio which should have the goal of preserving capital.

Third, use our trailing stop loss strategy that kicks out an ETF down 10% or so from its high.

Fourth, use put options to mitigate risk. When you buy the China ETF (FXI), consider buying a put option on this ETF out 18 months at the same time.

Fifth, if you have an emerging market ETF that has had a great run, why not take some money off the table? As old Joe Kennedy aptly put it: "only a fool holds out for top dollar".

My view is that for the most part, emerging market countries are in far better shape today than in the 1990s and valuations are not way ahead of themselves. Also some of the lower risk countries like Singapore are appealing. In the early part of 1997 before prices crashes, the Singapore Straits index was at 24 times earnings. Now it is 15 and the broader market is at 12 times earning.

Keep in mind that 200 years ago India and China made up 50% of world GDP. We have a long way to go with this story but you need a smart strategy able to weather some turbulence now and then.

Challenge the Indexes

When I called on global equity fund managers in Tokyo, Hong Kong and Sydney during the 1980s to pitch American small cap stocks, I was always struck by the leather covered ledgers they would pull out to jot down notes. No doubt the leather ledgers have been replaced by sleek computer notebooks and the time to meet with small cap stock pickers is probably also a thing of the past.

Why? The enormous size of many global equity funds would make even a ten bagger small stock hardly worth the trouble. Global fund managers need big cap liquid stocks and the larger funds have little choice but to take a top down approach in order to beat their benchmarks. This trend presents independent investors with a great opportunity to profit from following what country bets global asset managers are taking and even better, to ignore index weightings which are based largely on the size of a country's stock market rather than its growth prospects.

But first, let's discuss how a portfolio manger of a large global equity fund might approach his task of beating a benchmark such as the MSCI All Country World Index. This index weights 49 countries based on the market value of their stock markets. For example, the current index weights Japan at 11 %, the United States at 45.5 %, Australia at 2.3 %, Indonesia at 0.13 %, 0.37% and 3.1% in Germany.

To beat this benchmark, fund managers allocate assets differently. A manager may believe that a stronger yen and higher long-term interest rates may lead to a weak Japanese market and therefore underweight Japan. Or anticipate successful economic reforms in Indonesia or Germany leading to an overweight position.

Once the country allocation targets are established, fund managers then evaluate what companies they should invest in or another option is to use passive vehicles such as exchange-trade funds (ETFs) which track a country's stock market index.

Another method fund managers use in allocating assets is to divide the world into groups such as North America, Europe, Asia and emerging markets and then to weight countries within these categories differently than the benchmark. For example, in the MSCI Asia Index, Japan weighting is a surprising 68.6%, India is 4%, Singapore is 2.3%, while Indonesia is weighted only 0.78%.

Keep in mind that since some country stock markets and ETFs are dominated by just a few companies, an overweight or underweight allocation by fund managers will surely affect the price of these stocks. For example, Samsung Electronics () represents 20.8 % of the iShares MSCI South Korean ETF and BHP Billiton (BHP) accounts for 12.6% of the iShares MSCI Australia ETF.

If an investor can identify what countries or regions global fund managers are overweighting or underweighting, this intelligence could be used to weight their own individual global portfolios. In short, investors can react quickly to ride the coattails and anticipate where the global fund flows will move next.

Of course this strategy is not without its pitfalls. Strong domestic investment flows may offset or override international fund flows or unanticipated political events may tip markets either way.

Nevertheless, I view investing in countries with increasing international fund flows a little bit like running with the wind at your back. Taking positions in countries heavily underweighted by global equity funds is also a good value approach provided you have the patience to wait for the cycle to turn. All things considered, it's smart to know which way the wind is blowing.

Before making allocation changes to my portfolios, I check data from Emerging Portfolio Fund Research (EPFR) which tracks the trading activity of 10,000 funds worldwide representing $5 trillion of assets.

To me the MSCI country weightings are too backward looking. If you really want to your portfolio to outperform benchmarks in a big way, I suggest that you unshackle yourself from the country weightings. Look to the future and weight countries based on their growth potential and pace of market reforms. Follow the money and the growth for outsized returns.

Going Against the Grain

Sometimes it pays to draw an opposite conclusion from what seems to be overwhelming evidence. A recently released report, The New Global Challengers, published by the Boston Consulting Group, highlights how emerging-market companies are becoming major players in both developing and developed markets. The big markets of China, India and Brazil get the lions' share of attention. The real target for investors right now should be elsewhere.

Here are a few examples. Bharat Forge (India) is now the world's second-largest forging company. Embraer (Brazil) has surpassed Bombardier as the market leader in regional jets and Pearl River Piano (China) is the global volume leader in piano production.

The BCG study identified 100 of the largest companies with combined 2004 revenue of $715 billion that are based in ten emerging markets and are rapidly gaining global market share.

Asia is the home of 70 of these companies. China accounted for 44 of them, followed by India with 21 and Brazil with 12. Interestingly, only four of the Chinese companies on the list are privately owned while all the Indian companies on the list are publicly traded and have foreign strategic investors as stockholders. Only one of the Indian companies is state-controlled.

While China seems to dominate this list with more than double the numbers of run-ner up India, I believe that the state-ownership and control of most of the Chinese companies will be a severe handicap over the long haul. Some pundits argue that investors are better off investing in state-controlled Chinese companies because the gov-ernment will not allow them to fail. But this is offset by the likelihood that govern-ment ownership and control will limit their potential. Foreign governments may consider them an extension of the Chinese government and block their expansion into sensitive areas. State ownership will also lead to inefficiencies and an inability to hold onto top management talent.

This ownership and control issue plus India's advantages of having a democratic gov-ernment, a more youthful population and a well-developed stock market founded in 1870 is why you should favor India over China in your global portfolios. The problem is that the leading SENSEX index companies still seem a bit pricey. Investors need to reach down into the mid and small cap area for better value. You need exposure to the domestic economy and to names that aren't in the paper everyday and they also need to spread their risk.

While 77 of the 100 companies on the list were from China, India and Brazil, my instincts also led me to look at the bottom of the list where Indonesia has only one com-pany and Thailand and Malaysia have only two companies. Why not look beyond the headlines and hoopla and take a look at these countries?

Thailand, in large part due to its political problems, is one of the cheapest markets in the world with a market trading at just over seven times earnings not to mention that it is up so far this year 10.5%—twice that of the S&P 500. Indonesia is Asia's best performing stock market so far this year up 27%. Chartwell's portfolios use two closed-end funds for these markets, the Thai Fund (TF) and the Indonesian Fund (IF). It is a good idea to blend these in with high quality markets like Singapore (EWS), Australia (EWA), and Hong Kong (EWH).

Some analysts are questioning the potential rewards of investing in emerging markets because of their perceived higher risk. Meanwhile, as key central banks raise lending rates, bond yields are rising, and that makes riskier assets, such as emerging-markets stocks, look less attractive.

Go against the grain and build positions in higher quality emerging market countries and companies. Southeast Asia is being lost in the hype about India and China and presents global investors with a great opportunity.

Sometimes it pays to draw an opposite conclusion from what seems to be overwhelming evidence. A recently released report, The New Global Challengers, published by the Boston Consulting Group, highlights how emerging-market companies are becoming major players in both developing and developed markets. The big markets of China, India and Brazil get the lions' share of attention. The real target for investors right now should be elsewhere.

Here are a few examples. Bharat Forge (India) is now the world's second-largest forging company. Embraer (Brazil) has surpassed Bombardier as the market leader in regional jets and Pearl River Piano (China) is the global volume leader in piano production.

The BCG study identified 100 of the largest companies with combined 2004 revenue of $715 billion that are based in ten emerging markets and are rapidly gaining global market share.

Asia is the home of 70 of these companies. China accounted for 44 of them, followed by India with 21 and Brazil with 12. Interestingly, only four of the Chinese companies on the list are privately owned while all the Indian companies on the list are publicly traded and have foreign strategic investors as stockholders. Only one of the Indian companies is state-controlled.

While China seems to dominate this list with more than double the numbers of runner up India, I believe that the state-ownership and control of most of the Chinese companies will be a severe handicap over the long haul. Some pundits argue that investors are better off investing in state-controlled Chinese companies because the government will not allow them to fail. But this is offset by the likelihood that government ownership and control will limit their potential. Foreign governments may consider them an extension of the Chinese government and block their expansion into sensitive areas. State ownership will also lead to inefficiencies and an inability to hold onto top management talent.

This ownership and control issue plus India's advantages of having a democratic government, a more youthful population and a well-developed stock market founded in 1870 is why you should favor India over China in your global portfolios. The problem is that the leading SENSEX index companies still seem a bit pricey. Investors need to reach down into the mid and small cap area for better value. You need exposure to the domestic economy and to names that aren't in the paper everyday and they also need to spread their risk.

While 77 of the 100 companies on the list were from China, India and Brazil, my instincts also led me to look at the bottom of the list where Indonesia has only one company and Thailand and Malaysia have only two companies. Why not look beyond the headlines and hoopla and take a look at these countries?

Thailand, in large part due to its political problems, is one of the cheapest markets in the world with a market trading at just over seven times earnings not to mention that it is up so far this year 10.5%—twice that of the S&P 500. Indonesia is Asia's best performing stock market so far this year up 27%. Chartwell's portfolios use two closed-end funds for these markets, the Thai Fund (TF) and the Indonesian Fund (IF). It is a good idea to blend these in with high quality markets like Singapore (EWS), Australia (EWA), and Hong Kong (EWH).

Some analysts are questioning the potential rewards of investing in emerging markets because of their perceived higher risk. Meanwhile, as key central banks raise lending rates, bond yields are rising, and that makes riskier assets, such as emerging-markets stocks, look less attractive.

Go against the grain and build positions in higher quality emerging market countries and companies. Southeast Asia is being lost in the hype about India and China and presents global investors with a great opportunity.

Break the ETF BRIC

During the past year, investor interest in the so-called BRIC countries: Brazil, Russia India and China has skyrocketed with a commensurate rise in respective share prices.

Is it too late to jump on the bandwagon? What is the best way to invest in these countries and what allocations should be made to each country in the BRIC group?

Fund flows into BRIC countries have risen sharply during 2006 and these markets have bounced back nicely from the sharp June pullback. Interestingly, China has captured about half of all the net increases in investment from global equity managers. This BRIC mania has obscured three important basics about these markets.

The first is that these are without doubt less developed emerging markets with commensurate volatility and risk. If you got carried away in 2006, take some money off the table—now.

Second, your strategy for investing in these markets should be long term. The whole idea is that over time these faster growing markets will translate into above average returns but no doubt there will be lags and bumps along the way.

Third, it would be a mistake to view these four countries as just four cogs in a wheel. Each country has its own strengths and weaknesses and will probably not move together.

Russia for sure and Brazil to a lesser degree are essentially commodity plays. Russian share prices are highly dependent on energy prices and since all other indicators such as political freedom, manipulation of foreign investment, cronyism and market reforms are going the wrong way, I am highly skeptical of this market.

Brazil offers more hope but is also dependent on commodity prices since they account for 40% of all exports. President Lula's re-election this year may lead to more aggressive market reforms or a pullback which would inevitably lead to the familiar boom and bust cycle.

China and India are the most promising BRIC options. Both markets have been red hot and China is riding a super cycle of investment which may very well extend through the 2008 Olympics. It is clearly in the midst of building a world-class infrastructure in urban areas but the familiar risks such as its state-dominated economy, lack of any democratic reforms, and tensions in rural areas where the majority of Chinese still struggle might derail the prized "stability" so touted by the Communist leadership.

My view is that India over the long haul presents investors with the great bull market of the 21st century. India however, also faces daunting challenges such as how to finance the modernization of its woeful infrastructure given its high debt levels and ambivalence towards foreign investment and privatization? Another key issue is timing. Large cap Indian companies have had a terrific run and seem quite expensive at about 20 times earnings. If earnings stay strong in 2007, the market could strengthen, but if not, expect a sharp pullback.

The best way to invest in these BRIC countries is probably through low-cost, flexible, transparent exchange-traded funds (ETFs) and their kin—closed-end funds. Claymore introduced the first BRIC ETF this fall (EEB) which tracks liquid U.S. exchange-listed ADRs and GDRs. It should however be avoided since its top ten holdings account for 57% of the ETF's total exposure. In addition, 49% of its holdings are in Brazil, 31% in China, 14% in India and 6% for Russia.

You would be better off to make your own BRIC allocations based on your risk profile and investment objectives using country specific funds. One option is to use the China iShare (FXI), the Brazil iShare (EWZ) and the Morgan Stanley India Fund (IIF) as proxies for these markets. Barclay's is planning an ETN that will follow an index of the largest companies on the National Stock Exchange of India but this ETF will be market cap weighted.

I will wait to see the company weightings but will probably still prefer (IIF) because of its nice balance with the inclusion of several well respected Indian subsidiaries of world class multinationals such as Siemens and ABB. You need to carefully watch the premium that a closed-ended fund trades relative to its net asset value.

Where would I be right now in terms of a BRIC allocation? About 30% for China, 20% for India, 15% for Brazil, zero for Russia and 35% in cash.

BRIC investors have done very well this year. Take some of your gains and get your financial advisor a nice Christmas present.

ETF Currency Plays

After a year when higher American interest rates helped stem pressure on the U.S. Dollar, the currency is losing ground around the world. U.S. policy makers and investors are scrambling to cope with what may a long period of dollar weakness.

You don't have to go far to see evidence of the declining greenback—just look to Canada whose currency is at a twenty year high to the U.S. dollar. After bottoming out at 62 cents in 2002, the Canadian dollar known as the loonie has climbed to 90 cents and some predict parity.

It doesn't take an economist to understand this change of fortunes. While the U.S. is running enormous budget and trade deficits, Canada has recorded 10 straight years of balanced federal budgets, has one of the world's lowest national debts relative to GDP and, of course, is benefiting greatly from high commodity and energy prices.

The Canada iShare ETF (EWC) is up 47% over the last 12 months.

After showing some strength in 2005, the American dollar has also losing ground against the euro going from 0.79 euro to 0.82 euro during the last month

But it is in Asia that the American dollar faces its greatest challenge.

Pimco guro Bill Gross in his May Investment Outlook "As GM Goes, So Goes the Nation" advises investors to sell some U.S. assets and look at lower-cost, faster-growing countries in Asia that have higher savings and investment rates.

The finance ministers of Japan, China and South Korea issued a statement this week that announced "immediate launching of discussions on the road map for a system to coordinate foreign exchange policy" and the further study of a common currency unit.

While I am certainly not as fatalistic as Mr. Gross about the prospects for the American economy, since publishing in early 2003 The New Global Investor, I have called for investors to have an Asian tilt in their global portfolios.

Since ETFs are not hedged they are excellent investment tools to benefit not only from the appreciation of stocks held inside the ETF basket but also benefit from currency appreciation relative to the American dollar.

Here are a few examples. The Austria iShare (EWO) is up 57% over the past year, South Africa (EZA) is up 70%, Australia (EWA) is up 36%, Sweden (EWD) is up 39% and Singapore (EWS) is up 21%. Rydex has also introduced a Euro Currency Trust ETF (FXE) that would benefit from a stronger euro and has an annual fee of only 0.30%.

What does America needs to do to keep the dollar strong and maintain its premier status as a global reserve currency? First, show some fiscal discipline. President Bush should follow through on his veto threat if the $109 billion spending measure approved by the U.S. Senate this week passes the House. We have to start somewhere. The markets would also appreciate some sort of movement on entitlement reform because entitlements account for 79% of the national budget. In addition, nothing would help stir American innovation, growth and investment more than a flat tax.

A weaker American dollar directly translates into a lower standard of living for Americans. A weaker dollar may be seen by some as a way to spur exports and economic growth but in the end will lead to ruin. Let's make the tough fiscal choices now and avoid relying on growth choking higher interest rates alone to defend the value of the dollar.

Ryder Cup ETF Portfolio

Last time team Europe and team USA squared off, it wasn't pretty with America on the losing end of an 18 ½—9 ½ score. Later this week, the rematch is on in Kildaire,

Ireland and I hope the relative performance of European and American stock markets so far this year is not a leading indicator.

I will be glued to the tube during the matches pulling mightily for an American win but the home court advantage for team Europe will be tough to overcome. The European team is stocked with veteran players from the UK and Ireland complemented by players from Sweden and Spain.

Team Europe countries have certainly outshined the US in terms of investment returns this year. While the S&P 500 index is up 5.45%, the Spain ETF (EWP) is up 24.3%, Sweden (EWD) is up 19.2%, the UK (EWU) is up 18% and the closedended New Ireland Fund (IRL) is up 22%. The New Ireland Fund, managed by Bank of Ireland Asset Management, is close to a 52 week high and trades at a 5% discount to its net asset value.

Some of this out performance is due to stronger currencies. For Spain and Ireland, the euro is up 7.5% so far this year. Sweden opted out of the euro in 2003 and the Swedish Krona and the British Pound have also done well against the dollar. This is one of the benefits to investing in country-specific ETFs since they are not hedged against the US dollar.

There are many parallels between golf and investing. When I was an investment advisor with UBS, I frequently conducted popular investment seminars at golf clubs entitled, "Why Great Golfers Are Great Investors". Some of the points I made were that great golfers are well prepared and stick to a clear game plan, prize consistency and keep the ball in the fairway, carefully calculate the odds for every shot, have a team of talented coaches and caddies (your financial advisors) and, most importantly, keep their cool and get out of trouble with minimal losses.

American investors have a tendency to underestimate Europe and fall prey to the common perception of Europe as a slow-growth, bureaucratic, region offering minimal opportunities. This misses the point that Europe is host to many world-class multinationals that grab business all over the globe. For example, the fact that Germany is a slow growth economy spurs companies like Siemens and BMW to look for growth overseas.

In addition, investors need to recognize the pro-growth, less-regulated and market-oriented wing of Europe best represented by the UK and Ireland. Americans like to think of themselves as the leaders of global capitalism but perhaps we are getting a bit too complacent.

The Heritage Foundation/Wall Street Journal Index of Economic Freedom is an objective economic criterion that has been used for the last ten years to study and grade various countries.

The index is a careful analysis of the how free an economy is and measures 161 countries against ten broad factors of economic freedom. The findings of this study are straightforward: the countries with the most economic freedom also have higher rates of long-term economic growth and are more prosperous than are those with less economic freedom.

It might surprise you to learn that in the 2006 Index of Economic Freedom, Ireland ranks third, Luxembourg fourth, the UK fifth, and Denmark eighth. The United States tied for ninth place with Australia and New Zealand. Perhaps it's time for America to enact significant market reforms like the flat tax and start pushing back creeping overregulation.

My advice to investors is to enjoy the competition and support your home team while blending all the countries into your global portfolio. The beauty of golf is that both Ryder Cup teams will be playing on the same golf course and under the same conditions. The US team will need to be on the top of its game to beat team Europe. One thing is for sure, it cannot afford to be complacent.

Planes, Trains and Ships

With global trade booming, don't forget to look at the companies that move all that stuff around.

Corporate America's outsourcing to China's giant manufacturing platform and our 2005 record trade deficit may have you wringing your hands but it also represents opportunities for shrewd investors.

About 10% of America's GDP still represents manufacturing but an even higher 15% comes from the moving of goods and services (including imports) around the country and globe. A great play on this growth is the low-cost and tax-efficient iShares Dow Jones Transportation ETF (IYT) which is listed on the NYSE and has twenty holdings. This sector ETF is up % over the past 12 months and % so far this year.

Just over 19% of this basket contains Fed Ex and UPS and both companies are growing right with international trade. They are also helping companies improve service and cut costs through their consulting services. One example is work done by UPS for

Harley—Davidson Motor Company. Based in my hometown of Milwaukee since being founded in 1903, UPS found that Harley was making a lot of shipments of less-then-truckload size and it helped them develop a system to cross dock shipments in Chicago to consolidate shipments. It also recommended larger orders of parts and accessories to be sent directly to dealers thereby lowering costs and speeding up deliveries. Next on the agenda is improving international operations.

Another big part of the ETF is rail services provided by companies like Union Pacific, Burlington Northern Santa Fe and CSX. With our ports jammed with imports, railways are playing a key role moving them inland to consumer distribution points.

A shipper in the basket is Hawaii-based Alexander & Baldwin (ALEX) which was founded in 1870 and incorporated in 1900. Its largest subsidiary Matson is a leader in shipping between Pacific ports and Asia.

Then there is Expeditors International of Washington (EXPD), a global logistics company with 10,000 employees and nearly $4 billion in revenue. The company offers air and ocean freight forwarding services, insurance and distribution services and its stock has gone from a 52 week low of $47 to a current price of $86.

While you could invest in these companies individually, it makes sense to use this ETF for a convenient, inexpensive, and well diversified basket that should grow right along with the trains, planes and ships moving commerce both at home and around the world..

Asia Pacific

Japan

The Skeptical Japanese Investor

As the Japanese stock market is rocked and closed for the first time in more than 50 years, investors need to assess why the market has hit a speed bump and what comes next.

First, during the market's 42% rise in 2005, foreign investors were doing all the investing. The Tokyo Stock Exchange reported recently that through November, overseas investors purchased a net $81 billion in Japanese shares. This is a record and more than they purchased at the top in 1999. A recent Merrill Lynch survey also indicated that 62% of US fund managers were overweight Japan. This is saying a lot since Japan represents about 25% of the benchmark MSCI EAFE index and 50% of Asian stock market capitalization. Therefore, what looks like a market weighting to many looks like too big a bet on the Japanese market to me. Even in our Asian Opportunity portfolio we have never gone beyond a 25% weighting for Japan.

Second, Japanese institutional investors have been net sellers of Japanese equities and individual investors, while active traders, have only nibbled at the market. For example, a recent Wall Street Journal article reported that in October individual net purchases were only $1 billion. All signs point to the Japanese being traders not long term investors with full faith in Japan's economic recovery. One wonders whether the recent meltdown will make them more gun shy and trading oriented.

Third, an over reliance by foreign investors on the Japanese iShare that tracks the Nikkei 225 puts too much pressure on the vehicle as foreign investors head for the exits to lock in profits.

Fourth, the Japanese are classic momentum investors pushing values way beyond any reasonable values. Forget any fundamental analysis, if it goes up it attracts capital whether it is the Japanese, U.S. or Indian market.

In Japan, there is reality (one) and appearance (tatemae). Most of the news accounts I read emphasize all the positive trends and downplay the risks. Perhaps the Japanese are too gun shy after many false hopes but perhaps they see the reality clearer than we do.

Japan is a massive restructuring play and there are a lot of good signs. Banks are in much better shape, real estate prices are turning positive for the first time in 14 years, 2% economic growth is welcome after many years of stagnation, exports are strong and the successful Koizumi led reform efforts may indicate substantial change is on the way.

But still, Japanese may be thinking twice because they know the reality. Many firms will do well but the high flying growth of the past is gone. Exports to China are strong but both China and South Korea are right on their heels in terms of technology. High budget deficits together with a rapidly aging population mean tax hikes. Japan's bureaucrats are resisting reforms tooth and nail and many of the old ways will be incredibly hard to change.

The market may very well bounce back as foreign and Japanese investors keep faith in the Japan restructure story. My bet is that they will both be more conservative and look for domestic-oriented companies where there is still good value and less downside risk.

My advice: keep an eye on the Japanese investors and follow their lead.

Triangulate Japan

What's up or rather down with Japan? Here is why the Japanese market is drifting and why the bull story is still intact.

After a great 2005, the Japanese market as represented by the Nikkei 225 is down 3.3% so far this year. Relative to the global equity sell off, this is not bad but the weakness has soured interest in the Japan story.

At the World Money Show in January 2006, I anticipated this weakness since the great gains in 2005 were fueled by foreign investors and not the Japanese. In fact, Japanese institutional investors were net sellers in 2005 and Japanese retail investors only nibbled at the edges.

As 2006 opened, the majority of foreign money managers were overweight Japan which is saying a lot since Japan represents 65% of the Asia MSCI index. As these foreign flows of capital have slowed, Japanese investors have stepped up their investing in the Japanese market but at a slower pace. Therefore, the overall market is going sideways. Think of a bathtub with more water going down the drain then coming in at the spigot.

At some point later this year, I believe that overseas investors will come back searching for quality markets like Japan, Japanese investors will pick up their pace of buying plus M&A activity will also drive Japan's markets. This triangle of capital flows will re-ignite the Japanese bull market.

New corporate law introduced just last month will make it easier for foreign firms to convince Japanese shareholders that a merger with a foreign firm is in their best interest. Also, starting next May, foreign firms will be able to purchase Japanese companies in a M&A transaction with their shares rather than only with cash through a 100% owned Japanese subsidiary. This is referred to as a triangular merger. M&A activity in 2005 set a record with 2,713 transactions. Spin offs and restructurings will also increase.

Japanese corporate activity is robust with machine orders coming in today above optimistic expectations. Banks are lending and capital formation is building momentum. In February, bank lending showed positive growth for the first time in eight years.

The Japanese are also managing low-cost competition from countries like China better than America. While moving low-end manufacturing oversea, Japanese companies are holding on for dear life to the more profitable higher-end products and protecting R&D by keeping it at home.

Consumer spending which makes up 55% of GDP needs to quicken and that is why the behavior of the Japanese consumer and investor needs to watched like a hawk. Getting the first small and inevitable interest rate hike out of the way would also be a major plus for the market.

Keep most of your powder dry for now and if the Nikkei 225 index falls from the current 14,750 to below 14,000, I would see it as the time to begin building a significant position in the Japan iShare (EWJ).

If you choose to follow our ETF plus one strategy, I would recommend the financial services and securities firm Nomura (NMR) which is down 5.7% this year. At $18 a share, it is off its 52 week peek of $24 and will benefit from increased share trading and M&A activity.

Japan is back and has a rightful place in your global ETF portfolio but stay underweight the indexes and pick your timing carefully.

Japan's Comeback

As Prime Minister Koizumi prepares to turn over power to his likely successor Mr. Shinzo Abe, many are wondering what's next for Japan and the Japanese stock market. The next Prime Minister will step into a more powerful platform and will have the opportunity to build on the reforms put in place by the current administration. Under Koizumi's watch, the budget was slashed, bank bad loans were cleaned up, the post office privatized, and pork barrel politics reigned in. The privatization plan will be phased in with the Japan Post split into four companies in 2007, and its savings and life insurance services privatized in 2017. Japan Post has 262,000 employees and the great majority of post offices are run by "special postmasters" a position often passed down from father to son for generations.

Here is why the Japanese market is drifting and why the bull story is still intact.

After a great 2005, the Japanese market as represented by the Nikkei 225 is down % so far this year. Relative to the global equity sell off, this is not bad but the weakness has soured interest in the Japan story.

I anticipated this weakness since the great gains in 2005 were fueled by foreign investors and not the Japanese. In fact, Japanese institutional investors were net sellers in 2005 and Japanese retail investors only nibbled at the edges.

As 2006 opened, the majority of foreign money managers were overweight Japan which is saying a lot since Japan represents 65% of the Asia MSCI index. As these foreign flows of capital have slowed, Japanese investors have stepped up their investing in the Japanese market but at a slower pace. Therefore, the overall market is going sideways. Think of a bathtub with more water going down the drain then coming in at the spigot.

At some point later this year, I believe that overseas investors will come back searching for quality markets like Japan, Japanese investors will pick up their pace of buying plus M&A activity will also drive Japan's markets. This triangle of capital flows will re-ignite the Japanese bull market.

New corporate law introduced earlier this year make it easier for foreign firms to convince Japanese shareholders that a merger with a foreign firm is in their best interest. Also, starting next May, foreign firms will be able to purchase Japanese companies in a M&A transaction with their shares rather than only with cash through a 100% owned Japanese subsidiary. This is referred to as a triangular merger. M&A activity in 2005 set a record with 2,713 transactions. Spin offs and restructurings will also increase.

Real estate prices rose in Tokyo early this year for the first time in 14 years, corporate spending and exports are also moving in the right direction. The missing link is vigorous consumer spending which is trending upward slightly. Unemployment recently fell to a seven-year low and the Japanese are holding on to 40% of the world's $12 trillion in savings. Japanese corporate activity is robust with machine orders coming in today above optimistic expectations. Banks are lending and capital formation is building momentum.

The Japanese are also managing low-cost competition from countries like China better than America. While moving low-end manufacturing oversea, Japanese companies are holding on for dear life to the more profitable higher-end products and protecting R&D by keeping it at home. A national debt of $7 trillion and weak demographics are cause for concern but there is considerable optimism that Japan is getting past the fear of deflation and moving towards its former vitality.

Consumer spending which makes up 55% of GDP needs to quicken and that is why the behavior of the Japanese consumer and investor needs to watched like a hawk. Getting the first small and inevitable interest rate hike out of the way is also a major plus for the market.

It is time to begin building a significant but still underweight position in the Japan iShare (EWJ). If you choose to follow our ETF plus one strategy, I would recommend the financial services and securities firm Nomura (NMR) which is at $19.30 a share. It is trending upward and off its 52 week peak of $24 and will benefit from increased share trading and M&A activity.

Japan is back and has a rightful place in your global ETF portfolio.

The Japan ETF Export Proxy

With the Japanese economy and stock market back on track, Japanese trading companies with their deep historical roots and tentacles throughout the Japanese economy are worth a close look.

Japan's top four trading companies: Mitsui, Mitsubishi, Marubeni, and Sumitomo used to be the stars in the galaxy of Japanese economic clout. These behemoths trace their origins to the 1870s when Japan opened up to the world after two centuries of self-imposed isolation. Although they suffered during Japan's 14 year stagnation and all but disappeared from the American media's radar screen, they remain a powerful force and are an excellent proxy for Japanese growth. This is especially true since the surge in export growth has been the primary engine of Japan's economic recovery.

With strong earning momentum, improved balance sheets and rising commodity prices, the major trading companies are back where they belong at the forefront of Japan's overseas expansion. China has replaced America as Japan's largest trading partner and some analysts estimate that 19% of all Japan's overseas sales go to China.

My favorite is Mitsui & Company (MITSY) which was formed in 1947 but has links going back more than 300 years. To give you a feel for Mitsui's breadth and reach, it has 42 overseas subsidiaries and 88 overseas offices. The bull market in commodities prices has also been a boon for these trading companies and accounts for a substantial amount of their core business.

Mitsui also has the highest profit margins in the industry with net profits growing at double digit rates. According to Morgan Stanley which last week raised its target price for Mitsui 20%, it is trading at just under eleven times its 2006 earnings estimates and at a price of just 1.49 times book value. As usual, the Mistui & Co. (MITSY) ADR is trading at somewhat higher valuations but still represents good value relative to growth prospects.

With the Japanese consumer and investor still wary of the durability of the Japanese economic recovery, exports will have to carry it forward for the time being and Japanese trading companies are at the sweet spot of supporting export expansion. Together with the Japan iShare (EWJ) and Toyota (TM), Mitsui is a smart way to bet on Japan's resurgence.

Bold Koizumi, Bull Market

President Franklin Roosevelt often commented on how important it was to have the right enemies and to pick the right fights. Japanese Prime Minister Koizumi is in the fight of his life against the right enemy at the right time!

The issue is the privatization of Japan's powerful but inefficient postal service and the enemies are LDP party members that are blocking its passage. Prime Minister Koizumi stunned the political establishment by calling a snap election on September 11th with postal privatization front and center. He then had the audacity to recruit high profile candidates to replace the "obstructionists".

Why is the post office system so important? It is a blend of economics, politics and symbolism. With $3 trillion of assets, the 134-year-old postal system is a huge economic force and by privatizing it Koizumi hopes to unleash this liquidity, cut the bloated bureaucracy and lead the way to broader market reform. Prime Minister Koizumi is not coy about this stating: "privatization of the post office is the first step toward the reconstruction of Japan's politics and economy.

"It is political since the ruling Liberal Democratic Party (LDP) has longed used the postal system as its private bank for supporters, especially in rural areas. The party members and factions who oppose the Koizumi initiative have long been a thorn in his side and he has seized on the issue as a vote of confidence on his reform plan. Mr. Koizumi has pledged to step down if he loses the September 11th vote.

The privatization plan will be phased in with the Japan Post split into four companies in 2007, and its savings and life insurance services privatized in 2017. Japan Post has 262,000 employees and the great majority of post offices are run by "special postmasters" a position often passed down from father to son for generations.
This long overdue confrontation also highlights two realities long known by Japan watchers but ignored by the mass media.

The first is that Japan is to a great degree a socialistic country—in fact one of the few socialistic countries that have worked. Mr. Koizumi realizes that it is not working any more and is bent on opening it up and driving market reform. The second truth is that the key to economic reform is political reform and this means reducing the LDP's reliance on rural areas and making it more relevant to younger urban voters.

What does this all mean for investors? Japan's economy is already showing signs that a recovery is taking hold after a long period of deflation and weak growth. Real estate prices rose in Tokyo early this year for the first time in 14 years, corporate spending and exports are also moving in the right direction. The missing link is vigorous consumer spending which is trending upward slightly. Unemployment recently fell to a seven-year low and the Japanese are holding on to 40% of the world's $12 trillion in savings.

Japan's Nikkei rally during the past few months is welcome after it underperformed global markets for much of the year.

Since May, the index is up 13%. The Nikkei 225 index still trades at only about one-third its 1989 peak of 38,915 set in 1989. Foreigners now own 22% of the Japanese stock market and recently account for almost 40% of its trading activity. If and when Japanese investors re-enter the market, it will surely get a lift.

I predict victory for the Koizumi forces on September 11ᵗʰ and this will spark a further rally on Japanese markets—especially for undervalued domestic-oriented and smaller Japanese companies. Expectations are low for the Japanese market which is also a good sign.

Then there is the likelihood of a rise in the value of the yen from current 111 to the dollar to 100 yen or less offering American investors a potential currency gain. While this will hurt exporters, Japan imports almost all of its oil and a stronger yen will reduce its energy bill.

A simple and low cast way to invest in Japan is through the iShares MSCI Japan (EWJ) exchange-traded fund which captures 85% of Japan's publicly available shares. It is up just over 11% during the past year, offers broad diversification and an annual expense ratio of only 0.59%. Another great option is the no-load Matthew's Japan mutual fund or to gain exposure to smaller Japanese companies, try Fidelity's Japan Smaller Companies Fund (FJSCX) that is up 7.55% this year and 14% over the last 12 months. It has a 1.02% annual fee but be careful of 1.5% short-term trading fee for sales within 90 days of purchase.

The choice is yours—you can wait for September 11ᵗʰ to see if Koizumi's forces prevail or position your portfolio ahead of the victory and market rally.

Japan's iPod Secret

After a long winter, Japanese markets have reached a four year high with foreign investors doing the bulk of buying. Eager investors are clinging to the clean up of Japan's financial sector, an export surge to China and signs of a slight rebound in real estate prices and consumer spending.

But the painful period following the bursting of Japan's financial bubble obscured the core of Japan's economic vitality—manufacturing—and this has stayed strong and is gaining momentum.

Just look at Japan's current account surpluses over the past three years: $113 billion in 2002, $136 billion in 2003 and $172 billion in 2004. These numbers are remarkable against the backdrop of a yen that has risen more than 20% since early 2002 and almost 13% this year alone.

A majority of Japan's exports are manufactured goods and components. 50% of its exports to China in 2004 were electrical equipment and machinery and its top exports to the world include autos, electronic components, optical instruments, imaging equipment and computer parts.

Much is made over China's huge trade imbalance with America which reached $126 billion in the first eight months of this year. No doubt a sizable share of Chinese exports to America are chock full of Japanese components.

In addition, since components of products are made all over the world and then assembled somewhere else such as China for final shipment, it is hard to tell what country a product comes from. Take the tremendous success of the iPod with 30 million sold in the last four years. Apple was lionized for its creativity in getting the jump on Sony. But guess what? A Merrill Lynch report estimates that over 80% of the iPod's components were made by Japanese manufacturers.

While some of these components were made in offshore facilities, many were made in Japan which has been able to hold onto its industrial base better than America.

How do they do it? First, the Japanese continually moving up the value-added curve and are careful to keep the R&D and manufacturing of sophisticated components close to home while outsourcing the low end to low wage countries.

Secondly, even though China's wages are about 5% of Japan's, factory automation has lessened the importance of labor costs. For advanced high tech products it accounts for only 10-15% of total costs. Having manufacturing closer to home also shortens new product lead times and increases cooperation between R&D and production teams leading to a crucial edge in staying ahead of its nimble competitors.

Perhaps most importantly, having research, development and production closer to headquarters helps protect proprietary technologies.

Of course supporting these new products requires capital investment—a lot of it. This is a major reason the Japanese are adept at keeping their manufacturing prowess.

Canon is building a large digital camera facility in Japan and plans to spend 80% of its $7.2 billion capital budget in Japan over the next three years. This is a reversal from the past ten years when 80% of its capital budget was spent overseas. Toshiba is building a $2 billion semiconductor facility. Sharp, Matsushita and Nippon Steel are also building major plants in Japan.

Then there is Toyota Motors which is rapidly building capacity in its drive to become the world's largest automaker—a title that has been held by GM since 1931. This is six years before Toyota Motors was founded in 1937 as a spin off from a textile manufacturer. In its most recent quarter, Toyota boosted capital spending by 50% and Mr. Takeshi Suzuki, Senior Managing Director, recently stated that Toyota will spend $12.2 billion to increase capacity this fiscal year.

Canon, Sharp Hitachi, NEC and Toyota are all good plays on Japan's manufacturing edge while Sony will continue to lag until it boosts its R&D and catches up in product development. The Japan iShare (EWJ) exchange trade-fund is also an attractive option since it has about 50% exposure to Japan's manufacturing sector with an annual fee of only 0.59%.

And even though you may not go anywhere without your iPod, don't get too attached to the stock. It has had a good run on the back of stellar iPod sales but at 40 times earnings, its time to take some profits off the table and buy some more tunes.

Many of the attributes highlighted during the Japan boom in the 1980s such as its highly educated workforce, patient capital, pride in craftsmanship, loyalty, teamwork and discipline are all still in place. Investors can now hopefully profit from these skills being applied without excessive financial engineering.

China

China Portfolio Insurance

Are you excited about the upside potential of China but can't pull the trigger because of the significant downside risk? Here is a way to invest in China growth and still sleep at night.

China has been the largest economy in the world for eighteen of the past twenty centuries and it is clearly determined to regain its role as the hegemonic power in Asia and then challenge U.S. global leadership. Will it be able to sustain its 10% economic growth rate, quell rural discontent, build a sound market-based financial system, privatize dominant state-owned enterprises and move towards openness and democracy? This is a tall order and you can put me in the skeptic column.

Nevertheless, China's raw industrial power, momentum and the palpable ambition of the Chinese people could realistically yield a huge return.
I advise my clients to go ahead and invest in China but emphasize that this is a speculative investment. It is smart to protect against the considerable downside risk.

Here is a simple plan you might want to execute to capture the upside while cutting your losses if the Chinese economy hits a speed bump.

First, take a broad stake in China through investing in the China iShare exchange-traded fund (FXI) that is comprised of 25 of the largest and most liquid China names. All of the 25 stocks included in the China iShare are listed on the Hong Kong Stock Exchange. Some of them are incorporated in mainland China (H shares) and some of them are incorporated in Hong Kong (red chips). The China iShare has been picking up steam in the last few months and is up just over 12% so far this year.

The China iShare provides good exposure to three key sectors of China: energy (20%), telcom (19%) and industrial (18%). This concentration can be viewed as a plus or a minus depending on your perspective. For example, some smart investors are placing a bigger bet on China's consumer markets. The top five companies represent 40% of the index. The annual operating expenses of the China iShare are only 0.74% compared to 2% plus for other alternatives out there including actively managed China and greater China regional funds. Keep in mind that most of these companies are still largely controlled and owned by the Chinese government.

Next, take out some insurance to protect this position by purchasing a put option on the China iShare (FXI). It sounds complicated but is actually very straightforward. An option is a right to buy (call) or sell (put) 100 shares of a security on a fixed expiration date at a set price (strike price). For this right an investor pays a fee or premium.

While you may grumble about paying the premium with cold hard cash when you might not need it, you probably have home insurance just in case disaster strikes and no doubt you have some life insurance as well. Why not protect your portfolio as well? It is especially important to consider hedging against more risky emerging markets such as China. While countries like China offer tremendous upside potential, the downside risk can be daunting and immobilize even the bravest investor.

Let's look at a couple of examples. Say you buy 100 shares of the China iShare (FXI) which is trading at $62 per share. Your total exposure is $6,200. Then purchase a put option (right to sell the China iShare) that gives you the right to sell FXI at a price of $60 on the third Friday in January 2008. I think we all can agree that a lot could happen to

China, good and bad, from now until January, 2008. If the price of the China iShare moves down toward the strike price, the value of the option will increase.

This will cost you a premium of a little over $500 but limits your potential loss to $2 per share plus the premium. Or buy a put option at a strike price of $50 and your premium drops to about $200 with a worst case scenario of a loss of $12 per share plus the premium.

Here is another example. You know Latin American markets are hot and believe the bull market will continue but are wary that there is the potential for a sharp pullback. You could buy 100 shares of the Latin America 40 iShare (ILF) giving you exposure to Brazil, Argentina, Mexico and Chile at a price of $113 for a total exposure of $11,300. Then buy a put option giving you the right to sell 100 shares at a strike price of $100 in March 2006 for a premium of around $300. Your worst case scenario would then be a loss of 15% with unlimited upside.

Keep a cool head when investing in emerging market countries like China. They should represent only be a small portion of your portfolio and, whenever possible, take out some insurance.

Bank of America's China Blunder

I have a special interest in the Bank of America. My first job was with the Asia-Pacific group with the First National Bank of Boston, now part of Bank of America. I am also a shareholder and have recommended the stock through the Chartwell Advisor and other publications.

So I fell out of my chair when reading about Bank of America's recent decision to sell Bank of America (Asia) Ltd., its retail and commercial franchise in Hong Kong and Macao, to the state-owned and controlled China Construction Bank. What a terrible blunder.

Why on earth (or Pluto for that matter) would you trade a significant beachhead including 17 branches and assets of HK $49 billion that comes with preferred access into China's banking market for a paltry HK 9.7 billion ($1.25 billion) just 1.3 times book value?

For the answer, we need to look back to Bank of America's $3 billion investment in China Construction Bank in June, 2005. As part of the deal, Bank of America agreed not to compete on its own in mainland China.

This decision, which I publicly opposed at the time, put Bank of America's future in the hands of the China Construction Bank and by default into the hands of the Chinese government. Instead of leveraging its significant base in Hong Kong to build a brand and base in China, it will fade into obscurity.

Some defenders of this deal will no doubt point out that given China's state dominated business system, foreign banks have little strategic choice other than becoming minority partners with a big Chinese bank. This is a defeatist, defensive and short sighted strategy.

This all too common thinking assumes that it is smart to invest in and become a strategic partner with a state-owned entity like China Construction Bank because the Chinese Communist government will not allow it to fail. Perhaps, but they sure can change the rules. It also does not guarantee a superior rate of return.

Has the world just accepted without a fight that to do business with China they have to invest in or become partners with state-owned and controlled companies? Will China's ruling party get away with keeping control of its leading companies while reaping the profits from freely operating in the free enterprise global marketplace?

Bank of America should be the buyer of mainland Chinese banking operations, not the other way around. China Construction Bank has shrewdly gained from its partnership with the Bank of America. It has brought in much needed cash to shore up its balance sheet, enhanced credibility in the international marketplace, gained access to proven managerial talent and operational expertise, clipped the wings of a potential rival in mainland consumer banking, and has now acquired its Hong Kong and Macao assets.

China Starbucks Play

The effects of caffeine on the central nervous system were first discovered in the 6th century in the Ethiopian highlands by a sheepherder called Kaldi. After his sheep ate red berries from a coffee tree, they seemed a bit jumpy and had difficulty sleeping.

The berries next made their way to a local monastery where the Abbott made a drink by mixing the beans with water into a concoction that kept him alert through the long hours of evening prayer.

Coffee most likely made its way to Asia in the latter half of the 17th century when a Dutch trader brought a seedling from Yemen to Java where the soil proved hospitable leading to a thriving and profitable industry to this day. Vietnam is now the world's second largest coffee producer while India and Indonesia are in the top ten.

Despite substantial coffee production in Asia, much of the growth in the popularity of coffee in this predominantly tea drinking region can be attributed to instant coffee and the marketing efforts of Nestle. It rolled out the first commercially viable instant coffee in 1938 and it spread to Asia becoming a prestigious alternative to tea.

As incomes rose in Japan, coffee consumption grew as well making it the third largest consumer in the world. This is a trend that could continue in countries with rising disposable incomes such as China.

Coffee is now big business and as a world commodity is second to only oil.
This size and growth potential for a habit forming product like coffee sure sounds like an investment opportunity to me. But how should you play the rise of coffee in Asia.

Since it takes about 4-5 years for a coffee tree to bear cherries, investing on the production side is not for the faint of heart due to hard to predict coffee price fluctuations. As one of the largest coffee plantation companies in Asia, Tata Coffee Ltd. of India, is worth a good look especially since it is an integrated coffee company with roasting, exporting and retail operations.

Nestle is also a possibility since it is the leader in instant coffee in China and many parts of Asia. A drawback is that the coffee business represents only roughly 10% of the sales of this diversified food powerhouse.

The most attractive option is to invest in the retail coffee market which is highly fragmented. Starbucks (SBUX) is the global leader with 10,500 retail outlets of which 3,500 are outside North America. Starbucks began in Asia with its first store in Japan in 1996 and now has 165 stores in mainland China, 221 in Hong Kong, Taiwan and Macau, 595 in Japan, 64 in Australia and 34 in Singapore.

Thailand

Time Out for Thailand

You would think that as tanks roll into a capital in support a military coup that a country's stock market would tank as well. In Thailand it seems to be taken as business as usual and this is not exactly a compliment. The Thai stock market took no hit at all and is up 9.6% so far this year. The past year follows a scripted political pattern all too familiar to Asian hands.

Some cynics may make the case that an authoritarian government taking charge is good for investors. For short-term traders, this may be the case. But for serious long-term investors and for Thailand's economy and people, the cycle of new constitution, election, political paralysis, coup, and military takeover needs to be broken.

There have been 18 coups since the Kingdom of Thailand was established as a constitutional monarchy in 1932. The last coup was in 1991 and many hoped that the country had moved beyond its reliance on the military to sort out messy political patches.

After all, the now Prime Minister in exile Thaksin's party had won two elections decisively. Critics charge that he manipulated the system to consolidate power and when his family sold its controlling stake in a company in a way that led to no taxes on the proceeds, the seeds of rebellion were stoked.

It seems that holding an election is the easiest part of building a democratic form of government and that establishing an independent judiciary and protecting due process is the hardest and maybe the most important part.

The reason military coups happen so frequently in countries like Thailand is that the military is the strongest and most respected institution. Over the weekend, former Army Chief General Surayud Chulanont was formerly appointed interim prime minister. Thailand's military leaders also announced an interim constitution which sets out a nine-month timeline for drafting a new permanent constitution followed by new parliamentary elections. Who will be the drafters of the new constitution is not clear.

Instead of starting this cycle all over again, why not get to the bottom of the Thaksin controversy and bring closure to this unfortunate chapter? The current constitution may be just fine.

We also need to clear up what role the symbolic but powerful King of Thailand, Bhumibol Aduljadej who has reigned since 1946, played in the coup. In the past when the political temperature reached boiling point, a curt nod from the King was enough to send even the most imperious Prime Minister packing. This safety valve obviously did not work and the King may have pointed his next nod to trusted military leaders.

Meanwhile, this political instability has cost Thailand dearly in terms of foreign investment and economic growth. With a land area more than twice the size of Wyoming, Thailand is a youthful solid middle-income country with a consumer-oriented middle class. Its economy is well diversified, is rich in natural resources, and has a vibrant manufacturing sector and strong exports.

The Thai stock market is one of the cheapest markets in the world trading at just seven times earnings. Even so and my strong belief in the country's potential, I am taking a time out before looking at the closed-end Thai Fund (TF) managed by Daiwa Securities. History shows that that the Thai market is both resilient and explosive. Thailand's benchmark SET index rose 115% in 2003.

Foreign investors may be jumping in but Thai citizen's patience with the cycle of instability may be wearing thin.

A Nod from the King

Thailand's Prime Minister Thaksin Shinawatra resignation this week is a major opportunity for investors willing to step into a temporary political vacuum.

The Prime Minister's surprise announcement came after a meeting with the symbolically powerful King of Thailand, Bhumibol Aduljadej, at his seaside palace. The King has presided over Thailand since 1946 and is revered by all.

As in the past when the political temperature reaches boiling point, a curt nod from the King is enough to send even the most imperious Prime Minister packing. This safety valve is a key part of Thailand's constitutional monarchy which helps it to maintain stability in times of a crisis.

Investors should not stay on the sideline until a new premier is selected when parliament resumes within the next 30 days but should act now to take advantage of an undervalued Thai market.

With a land area more than twice the size of Wyoming, Thailand is a youthful solid middle-income country with a consumer-oriented middle class. Its economy is well diversified, is rich in natural resources, and has a vibrant manufacturing sector and strong exports.

While many Asian markets such as Hong Kong, Singapore and Japan are hitting multi-year record highs, the Thai market has lagged due largely to the political turmoil. GDP growth for 2006 should match or better last years 4.5% number and fuel subsidies have been cut relieving pressure on the national budget. International capital flows to Thailand remained stable during the crisis but will likely ramp up quickly once calm is restored.

History shows that that the Thai market is both resilient and explosive. Thailand's benchmark index rose 115% in 2003.

I suggest investors use the closed-end Thai Fund (TF) managed by Daiwa Securities which is trading at a 2% premium with a share price of $9.75 down from a 52-week high of $11.32.

The King has acted, so should you.

Singapore

Singapore Firing on All Cylinders

You can always count on Singapore Inc. to have a forward-leaning plan plus the talent and will to execute it. Looking to spur growth and reduce its dependency on cyclical industries like electronics and manufacturing, Singapore's goal is to become Asia's hub for life sciences and financial services.

To succeed in the competitive arena of life sciences and, in particular, biotech, a country needs five ingredients: talented scientists, strong corporate partnerships, resources to back R&D, protection of intellectual property and top-notch facilities.

It is searching the globe for talent and offers big bucks for coming to Singapore to conduct research. Alan Coleman, who led the team of geneticists that cloned a sheep, received a $6 million grant to relocate to Singapore. Edison Liu, former head of clinical sciences at the U.S. National Cancer Institute, left to head up the Genome Institute of Singapore.

The government of Singapore is also supporting life sciences with ample resources. Big Pharma companies such as Merck and Eli Lily are already active in Singapore; corporate partnerships such as the Singapore-based Novartis Institute for Tropical Diseases are also important for establishing credibility, using resources and attracting talent. Protection of intellectual property is a high priority for companies conducting biotech research. This plays to another of Singapore's strengths: It has been ranked by the Political and Economic Consultancy (PERC) as having the best intellectual property right protection in Asia since 1997.

For facilities one needs to look no further than Singapore's bio-medical facility Biopolis. Its first phase, 2-million-square-foot complex was completed in 2004. It has tenants such as Singapore's major bio-medical institutions, Johns Hopkins Singapore's bio-medical division and companies like GlaxoSmithKline. It has a computing room that can house a petabyte of data storage as well as incubators for startups.

All this activity has also spawned some home-grown biotech companies. Nextwave Biomedical is a privately held company that has built a prototype to analyze DNA in the field to speed up detection of diseases such as dengue and bird flu. Biosensors International Group, (BIG, S$1.10), listed on Singapore's Main Board, is well-positioned to become a leader in drug-eluting stents as opposed to traditional therapy options such as metal stents and open heart surgery. The company has developed drug-eluting stents made of a polymer material that is absorbed by the body. Since going public last May, Biosensors is up 57%. The company manufactures in Singapore, the Netherlands and China.

It is difficult to become Asia's financial hub without a thriving well-regulated stock market. The Singapore Exchange (SGX, price TK) went public in 2000 and is listed on its own bourse. The World Economic Forum's Global Competitiveness survey issued in 2005 included a section on regulation in securities exchanges. Among the 104 securities exchanges covered, Singapore ranked tenth. In the Asia-Pacific region, only Australia and New Zealand score higher.

SGX has made steady progress in expanding and globalizing its listings. In fiscal 2005 ending in June, it added 80 new listings including its first Indian and Israeli company. More than a quarter of all listings are foreign companies of which Greater China companies account for over 70%.

The financial numbers for SGX have also been impressive. In fiscal 2004, its return on equity was 20.8% rising to 23.1% for fiscal 2005. An investor would have been better off over the past three fiscal years investing in SGX rather than tracking the prestigious Straits Times Index. The annualized total shareholder returns over the 2003-2005 fiscal years was 35.7% for SGX versus 16.3% for the Straits Times Index.

For the first half of the fiscal year ending in June 2006, after-tax net profits were the highest since SGX went public. SGX is a great proxy for Singapore but another option is the Singapore iShares (EWS) exchange-traded fund, which was up 17.4% over the last 12 months.

While the Singapore market has had a good run, it does not seem overvalued to me. According to data from Thomson Financial, the Straights Times Index trades at 15 times earnings, far from levels in 1997 when it was overextended at 24 times earnings.

I view Singapore as the Switzerland of Asia and a great core holding for your global portfolio.

India

India Beats China as Next Great Bull Market

India has the potential to be the next great bull market of the 21st century—an opportunity of being a better investment than even China!

Like China, India was stuck with a failed economic system for over 50 years. It was a bureaucratic, socialist state that led to weak growth, and stymied entrepreneurship and initiative. Famines, lack of investment, and poverty were the result.

But In the early 1990's, the country changed course and started to open up its economy to the world. Personal marginal tax rates have fallen from 50% to less than 30%. Tariffs and import quotas were slashed, exports are growing at a 20% annual rate, with America being its largest market. Only 10% of its economy is dependent on international trade, insulating it somewhat from external shocks. The banking system is much improved, and non-performing loans have dropped to less than 4% of total bank loans. It has fiscal crisis to accumulating $135 billion in foreign exchange reserves.

Here are six reasons that investors should consider tilting some of their long-term capital towards India and not China.

Unlike China, India is a functioning democracy with respect for property rights and the rule of law. China's authoritarian state may have the advantage at making quicker decisions and pushing through economic reforms but without democratic political reform it will eventually hit a speed bump the size of the Great China Wall. India's multi-party parliamentary system with its obstructionist bureaucracy is far from ideal but at least the daily speed bumps on the road to market reform can be overcome.

India is a natural ally of the U.S. as it emerges on the global stage and plays classic balance of power politics. America's relationship with China will at best be wary and tense. The fact that many Indian citizens speak English is also a significant advantage both commercially and politically.

China's state-owned companies have staying power but government ownership will limit their growth and potential. Foreign governments will be suspicious of their intentions and likely consider them as an extension of the Chinese government. State ownership will also lead to inefficiencies and an inability to hold onto top management talent.

India's capital markets are better than China's. India's stock market was established in 1870 and has 6,000 publicly-traded companies and a more modern financial and banking system that allocates capital fairly well. Only 10% of bank credit in China goes to private companies. India has 100 companies with a market cap over $1 billion.

India is a very youthful nation with 50% of its population under 25 years of age. This leads to less strain on its national budget and the hope that the younger generation will drag the bureaucracy and politicians to swifter implementation of market reforms. China's one-child policy has backfired leading to an aging population which will lead to manpower shortages and tremendous pressure on its national budget. 20% of Shanghai residents are over 60 years old and by 2020, one-third of Shanghai's population of 13.5 million will be over 60.

India has a more balanced and sustainable economy with 64% of its GDP attributable to consumer spending and 50% of its GDP from service sector. China's economy is more dependent on foreign investment, exports and resources. India's 250 million living in poverty is a tragedy but it's middle class has quadrupled during the past two decades to reach 250 million as well.

For sure India has its challenges: big infrastructure needs, frustrating red tape and a tendency for the government to hang on to large state-owned enterprises to mention a few. It has recently suspended its privatization program, has high levels of public debt, very poor basic services such as elementary education, water and health, rigid labor laws, and still lacks the consensus that exists in China for welcoming foreign investment and placing a high priority on economic growth. India's infrastructure such as roads, power and ports is also in desperate need for investment. This is one area that China is way ahead of India. The other is China's ability to attract roughly ten times as much foreign direct investment.

India's economy is doing well but is still below its potential. Just think if India embraced foreign investment, privatization, had the political will to improve the lives of workers in agriculture by consolidating farms and using more technology to vastly improve productivity. If it can provide its citizens with quality basic education and other services and put in place adequate power and other infrastructure, it can create 100 million new jobs in industry and manufacturing.

Still, compared to China, India does not get much attention except for the outsourcing issue and is—for now—largely under the radar screen of even sophisticated investors. After a strong start this year, India's 30 company Bombay Sensitive Index (Sensex) index was beaten down more than 20% but has recovered to be flat for the year.

The challenge with investing in India right now is valuations of the leading companies and the limited investment options. Valuations may be getting a bit ahead of themselves with SENSEX companies trading at around 17-18 times next year's earning projections versus 13 times for emerging markets as a whole.

The Morgan Stanley India Fund (IIF) is a closed-end fund that invests in India's blue chips trading at $42, quite a bit off its 52-week high of $57. It is a bit pricey right now and trades at a 17 % premium to net asset value so caution is recommended until this premium comes down to the historical average in the low single digits. I would make only a modest allocation at this point. There are also some Indian ADRs trading on U.S. exchanges and these are also expensive and trade at a price premium over the India market price. My favorites are Dr. Reddy's Laboratories (RDY), HDFC Bank (HDB) and Tata Motors (TTM).

Be patient—there no doubt will be great investment opportunities as well as new investment vehicles to take advantage of this great secular bull market.
India presents investors with the opportunity of a lifetime and its democratic government, stronger financial system, market-based interest rates and history of respecting property and intellectual rights may make it a better long-term play than China.

Asia's New Investment Jewel

Let's discuss an Asian country that could present us with the next great bull market of the 21st century—an opportunity that has the potential of being a better investment than even China!

Like China, this country was stuck with a failed economic system for over 50 years. It was a bureaucratic, socialistic state that led to weak growth, and stymied entrepreneurship and initiative. Famines, lack of investment, and poverty were the result.

But In the early 1990's, the country changed course and started to open up its economy to the world. The country's personal marginal tax rates have fallen from 50% to less than 30%. Tariffs and import quotas have been slashed, exports are growing at a 20% annual rate, with America being its largest market. Only 10% of its economy is dependent on international trade, insulating it somewhat from external shocks. The *banking system is much improved, and non-performing loans have dropped to less than 4% of total bank loans. It has quickly gone from a balance of payments deficit to accumulating $135 billion in foreign exchange reserves.*

Unlike China, it is a functioning democracy with respect for property rights and the rule of law. Many of its citizens have English as their native language. It also has more advanced financial markets than China, and a stock market established in 1870 that has 6,000 publicly-traded companies.

It is a very youthful nation with 80% of its population under 45 and—this is amazing—25% of all people 25 and under in the world live in this one country! Its Citizens are thrifty with money to spend with a 28% savings rate to support capital investment. Consumer finance is rapidly becoming available and fueling more consumption and retail sales totaled $180 billion last year.

Economic growth is already impressive with 8.2% last year and 7% projected for 2005. Per capita GDP adjusted for prices is higher than China and its GDP growth rate has averaged 6% during the past 10 years. Fifty percent of its output comes from services and it has world class IT, media advertising, entertainment and pharmaceutical expertise.

The country's space program has launched 12 consecutive rockets without incident and it put the world's first graphic mapping satellite into orbit earlier this year. It has become a close ally of the United States recently signing a defense pact and placing a huge order with Boeing while considering purchasing advanced F-16 and F-18 fighters. President Bush, not a big traveler, is planning to underscore the importance of strong bi-lateral ties by visiting this country by the end of this year.

You have probably guessed by now that the country we are discussing is India—the world's largest democracy.

For sure India has its challenges: big infrastructure needs, frustrating red tape and a tendency for the government to hang on to large state-owned enterprises to mention a few. Still, compared to China, India does not get much attention except for the outsourcing issue and is—for now—largely under the radar screen of even many sophisticated investors. India's 30 company Bombay Sensitive Index (Sensex) index is up 22% this year and broke the 8,000 barrier just last week. Much of the buying is being done by foreign institutional investors from the U.S., and more recently, Japan.

The challenge with investing in India right now is valuations of the leading compa-nies and the limited investment options. Valuations may be getting a bit ahead of themselves with Sensex companies trading at around 14-16 times next year's earning projections versus 11 times for emerging markets as a whole.

The Morgan Stanley India Fund (IIF) is a closed-end fund that invests in India's blue chips and is up 97% in the last 12 months and 39% so far this year. It is a bit pricey right now and trades at a 14% premium to net asset value so caution is recommended until this premium comes down to the historical average in the low single digits. There are only eleven Indian ADRs trading on U.S. exchanges and these are also expensive and trade at a price premium over the India market price. One exception may be Tata Motors (TTM) which is listed on the NYSE at a price of $11.50, has a dividend yield of 4% and trades around 13 times 2006 consensus earnings estimates.

Where to act right now? For the right investors, there are long-short funds that focus more on India's small and mid-sized companies which tend to be much better values, have not participated in the recent run up of prices and are also more insulated from global capital flows. These funds can also hedge against companies with unsustainable valuations and cushion inevitable pullbacks in the market. Be patient—there no doubt will be great investment opportunities as well as new investment vehicles to take advantage of this great secular bull market.

India presents investors with the opportunity of a lifetime and its democratic govern-ment, stronger financial system, market-based interest rates and history of respecting property and intellectual rights may make it a better long-term play than China.

South Korea

Samsung the Elephant

Samsung dominates life in its home country like no other company in the world. But the slogan "what is good for Samsung is good for South Korea" is open for debate.

The South Korean economy is a paradox. It has become the third largest economy in Asia after Japan and China. Its 48 million citizens have in one generation enjoyed a sizable jump in their standard of living and no country has benefited more than South Korea from the rise of China which has become a vital export market. Its sovereign credit rating was recently upgraded due to reduced tensions with North Korea and it enjoys foreign exchange reserves of over $200 billion. It just posted a better than *expected third quarter with GDP growth of 4.4% year-on-year spurred by higher than anticipated exports and consumer spending.*

The Korean people should be full of satisfaction for a job well done but instead are rather a discontented lot.

Why? Its per capita income is still about one third that of the OECD average. Expected economic growth of about 3% is closer to a mature economy than an Asian tiger and Japan's economy is still six times larger. Unemployment is becoming an issue and a stronger currency and relatively high wage levels are crimping exports which account for 40% of its economy. Exports are up 8% this year after a 31% jump last year. After a credit card binge, average net consumer borrowing is equal to 100% of disposable income and the bank of Korea recently bumped up its benchmark rate for the first time in three years.

What is going on here? Somewhat surprisingly, South Korea is experiencing many of the same outsourcing issues that Americans complain about. It was the largest investor in China last year with over $6 billion in fixed investments. Its largest steel maker POSCO announced its intention to invest $12 billion in a steel plant in India where it already runs 24 steel companies. Hyundai manufactures 600,000 autos in China and its affiliate Kia makes 150,000 more.

Meanwhile Samsung Electronics has become Asia's largest technology company by market cap (larger than Sony), and its largest maker of memory chips and flat panel screens and mobile phones. Samsung enjoys a credit rating higher than South Korea's sovereign rating. With 62 affiliates, the Samsung group dominates life in Korea like no other company in history. It represents 15% of the nation's total economic activity, 25% of the capitalization of the KOSPI stock market and the taxes it pays represent almost 10% of total government income!

Samsung, up 25% so far this year, is still attractive at about 11 times consensus 2006 earnings estimates and its operating profit was up 29% in the third quarter. Despite third quarter net income declining 30%, a strong fourth quarter is expected. There is a shortage of LCD television panels and its flash memory chip global market share exceeds 60%. As prices have come down flash chip sales have gone up 40%.

But the company is not a terrific play on the South Korean economy. Rather it is a global play on its three key markets and the expected payoff from its extraordinary commitment to R&D. The South Koreans are discontented because the five largest companies are growing outside the country more than in it and at a stage of development where it should be more competitive manufacturing onshore. The challenge is the low cost manufacturing platform with huge economies of scale just next door—the issue is China. Samsung already has already has 29 plants and 50,000 workers in China.

Since China is already starting to manufacture stuff like machine tools that the South Koreans were busily exporting in 2003 and 2004, South Korean planners believe it must quickly transform itself into a finance, communications and transportation hub—akin to the role of Singapore or Switzerland. The question then becomes does it have the right companies, the right skills and what is its competitive advantage?

Together, Samsung, POSCO, KEPCO (Korea Electric Power) and SK Telecom account for almost 50% of South Korean stock market's market capitalization. To use a basketball analogy, the South Korean starting five are strong but its bench is a bit thin and its team has lost the home court advantage. The problem is not Samsung but rather that they need about ten more Samsungs.

The top four companies also make up 40% of the South Korea iShare (EWY) ETF which is up 29% so far this year. Samsung alone accounts for 23% of this ETF and buying the iShare gives you more exposure to the top ten South Korean companies. A smart move would be to take advantage of the strong third quarter and take some profits off the table. The stronger won and higher interest rates will lead to slower growth and the likely re-emergence of the North Korean problem may very well undermine investor confidence.

Bottom line: buy Samsung based on valuation and top notch global reach and R&D but expect tougher going for the South Korean economy as China turns from robust export market to direct competitor.

Australia

Surfs Up Down Under

The lucky country's economy is on a record-breaking 14 year roll. The question is: will it continue?

Just imagine, from a few convicts dropped ashore in 1788 Australia has developed into a first class global economy. The reforms enacted by former Prime Minister Bob Hawke and Treasurer Paul Keating during the 1980's set the stage for a remarkable run of prosperity. Specifically, they slashed import tariffs, floated the currency and reduced the power of big labor. The current Prime Minister, John Howard who has been elected for times, has continued and expanded these reforms riding a wave of economic growth—14 years of uninterrupted 4-5% growth.

The national debt has virtually been eliminated, the currency strong, the government recently signed a free-trade pact with America and is starting to negotiate a pact with China. Australia received $42 billion in foreign direct investment in 2004.
This is all great news and our portfolio allocation to the Australia iShare (EWA) has done very well with a 105% gain over the past two years. The Australian iShare is up 15% so far this year and provides investors with exposure to about 60% of the total stock market.

The question is of course, what should we do now? When things are going this well for so long investors need to be skeptical and weigh the potential upside with the downside risk.

Despite all of Australia's strengths, there are some areas of concern:

- *there is a shortage of skilled and semi-skilled workers and relatively high labor costs (minimum $400 a week)*
- *complicated and rigid labor rules continue to hamper productivity growth which seems to be slowing*
- *the total tax take by the Australian federal government is 22% which is higher than the rest of Asian competitors and US (average of 16%)*
- *from 2000-2004 housing prices were up 100% and household debt is now 160% of disposable income*

Australia is taking some measures to address these issues. It recently enacted a $17 billion cut in personal income taxes over three years and the independent central bank is raising rates. The leadership has also introduced a package of "radical" labor reforms which if enacted would also be a big plus. The aim is to give employers more flexibility and to bring labor negotiations down to the local level. The measures would increase probationary period for new employees from 3 to 6 months, exempt businesses with less than 100 employees from unfair dismissal laws and favor individual contracts over collective bargaining. All of these measures will be fought by the Labor Party and trade unions.

While much is made of Australia's dependence on China and commodity exports, the Australian economy is well diversified with 5% of GDP attributed to mining, 5% to tourism and 80% to services. It also represents the third largest stock market in the region and a leading regional financial center.

After looking closely at the situation, I have decided to keep Australia in our portfolio but take some profits by halving our position. Here is my reasoning:

- *the decline in housing prices has been incremental and has therefore not impacted banking, consumer and construction stocks as expected*
- *international fund managers are underweight Australia*
- *the market is not especially expensive—12-month forward p/e ratio is about 15x, in line with average over past three years and below high of 18x. However, keep in mind that this low multiple is based on forward and aggressive forecasts of corporate profits.*
- *average dividend yield for Australian stocks is around 5%*

One company to keep an eye on is BHP Billiton (BHP), the world's biggest mining group, which reported an 85% rise in net profit compared with a year ago, to $6.5 billion, for the year ending June 30th. The Anglo-Australian firm set a new Australian corporate profit record and after being up sharply in 2003 and 2004 has confounded skeptics by being up 26% so far this year. The company's good fortune, like that of other mining concerns, comes from rising demand in China. Another great Australian mining company is Rio Tinto which has a lower valuation because it doesn't have oil & gas operations that contribute about 30% of BHP's total revenue.

The center of gravity of the world's economy is shifting to the Asia-Pacific region and Australia is in the sweet spot. Keep an eye on housing prices and corporate profit performance but for now keep some exposure to Australia in your global portfolio.

Taiwan

Calling China's Bluff on Taiwan

Politics not economics is usually the first concern for most investors considering investing in Taiwan. For the next couple of years, both lead to a window of opportunity for investors with nerve and foresight.

There is little doubt that for the leadership of the Chinese Communist Party, Taiwan is a bone in their throat—a constant irritant—and most likely an obsession for some hard-line factions determined to bring Taiwan back into the fold of the motherland. So sensitive is the issue that an uproar ensued when Google deleted the words "Taiwan, a province of the People's Republic of China" during a recent routine update of its online map of Taiwan

Even so, any noise that Beijing will take near term military action against Taiwan is likely a bluff for five reasons.

First, any military conflict with Taiwan would surely cancel the Beijing's showcase 2008 Olympics. This would be a devastating setback for China's leadership and people

Second, Beijing's approach of working quietly to support more friendly political factions within Taiwan seems to be working. In the municipal elections held on December 3rd, the so called "Pan Blue" coalition, composed of parties more flexible regarding reunification with China than the ruling party, captured 17 out of 27 seats building on the coalition's success in the 2004 legislative election. In addition, Taiwanese President Chen Shui-bian's term will end in 2008 and Beijing is betting on a less strident and independent successor.

Third, although China is rapidly modernizing its military forces, U.S. treaty obligations to Taiwan in the event of an invasion cannot be discounted. In addition, President Chen, citing China's expanded missile program in his annual New Year's Day address, called for the legislature to approve plans to purchase more weapons from the U.S. to offset the buildup.

Fourth, a 2005 joint statement by the Japanese and U.S. governments that both countries had a "common strategic objective" to "encourage the peaceful resolution of issues concerning the Taiwan Strait through dialogue," raises the possibility of Japanese intervention making the military option even more risky and improbable.

Lastly, the economic integration of Taiwan into China is moving ahead at a breathtaking rate. Cross-Straits trade has doubled since 2000 to reach $62 billion in 2004, about 1 million Taiwanese have re-located to work in China, and Taiwanese companies now account for about 65% of hardware output from the mainland.

My view is that while calls for independence have at least temporarily been muted, the desire for a high degree of autonomy from China is still strong. There may be one China but there are three systems—China, Hong Kong and Taiwan. Perhaps the best solution is for China and Taiwan to formally agree to a long period of Taiwanese autonomy to see if China's system evolves into a more open, transparent system with rule of law and democratic institutions.

Taiwan with a population of 23 million and an area of 14,000 square miles (half the size of Ireland) is a remarkable success story. However, but Taiwanese companies will

*need to constantly innovate, make Taiwan a major R&D center and build strong con-
sumer brands to avoid the it's economy from being swallowed by the mainland.*

*If you can get over the political risk and are ready to call China's bluff, Taiwan's stock
market represents good value though you should expect some volatility. In his New Year's
Day address, President Chen also called for Taiwan to maintain and nurture a separate
identity and renewed his pledge to have a new constitution in place before he leaves
office in 2008. Concerns about the remarks impact on China relations led the next day
to Taiwan stocks day falling 1.3% but the next day the market promptly bounced back
2% to reach a twenty month high as investors focused on economic fundamentals. The
laptop maker Wistron alone rose the daily 7% limit to an all time high.*

*Taiwan's stock market was up only 6% in 2005 lagging Asian markets such as Japan,
up 42% and South Korea, up 54%. One company that had a great year is Taiwan
Semiconductor (NYSE: TSM) which was up over 35% and still looks like a buy. It
has a return on equity of 16%, a strong balance sheet and a low level of institutional
ownership.*

*If you want more diversification, you should invest in the iShares Taiwan (EWT)
exchange-traded fund. It has a 23% exposure to the semiconductor industry and
Taiwan Semiconductor accounts for 14% of its holdings but it includes significant
exposure to technology hardware, materials and banks.*

*In 2005, Japan, Australia and South Korea were the most successful China plays. In
2006, why not take some profits and place a bet on Taiwan, also known legally as the
Republic of China.*

New Zealand

Follow the Kiwi

*Is New Zealand more than just a great place to visit and live? Australia gets a lot of
attention in the investment community as a play on commodities and China's economic growth but its neighbor seems off global investor's radar screens.*

*Let's take a look at the New Zealand stock market, economy and currency and see if
the time is right to take a stake in this beautiful corner of the world.*

First, the New Zealand stock market (NZX) is not very large or liquid. Its total market capitalization as of late 2005 was $42 billion compared to $778 billion for the Australian market. Of the top twenty companies by weight on the NZX, five are headquartered in Australia (Promina, Goodman Fielder, Westpac, APN News and ANZ Bank) and one (GPG) in London. The top ten New Zealand company listings on the market represent 57% of the New Zealand company market value. This is heavily concentrated in its top three listed companies: Telecom New Zealand (TEL) representing 29% of New Zealand company market value, Fletcher Building Limited (FBU) at 15%, Contact Energy (CEN) at 14% and Auckland International Airport (AIA) at 8%.

Furthermore, the New Zealand market was hit very hard by the 1987 stock market crash and still trades below those levels excluding dividends. At that time many listed companies went under and distressed banks ended up in Australian hands. The New Zealand market also does not benefit from the steady fund flows from Australia's compulsory savings program that boosts Australian share prices.

Still over the past six years, the per capita income of New Zealand's 4 million citizens has been steadily rising to climb over $24,000 (USD). Its economy has become more balanced with industry and services growing to account for the majority of economic activity but agriculture and in particular, dairy produce, still play a key role especially since exports comprise 22% of GDP. It is difficult to invest in the dairy sector because almost all dairy produce is sold to a national co-operative.

Unfortunately, during the past year the New Zealand economy has slowed and is likely to slow further. A sizable current account deficit is also approaching 10% of GDP. This brings us to the issue of the New Zealand dollar better known as the kiwi. The kiwi has been getting a lot of attention recently because investors such as hedge funds have been borrowing at low rates in currencies like the Japanese Yen and then buying NZ dollar assets to get at its higher interest rates. The kiwi recently reached a seven-month high against the US dollar and the currency seems overvalued to me. Even New Zealand's finance minister Michael Cullen has called taking a bet on the NZ dollar "slightly strange" cautioning investors that history shows that the kiwi "can move fast and a long way." When the NZ dollar starts moving the other way, it could turn into a stampede if hedge funds all bail out at the same time.

So there we have it, a slowing economy, an overvalued currency and a small and not very liquid market. Where are the opportunities? Now is not the right time but investors should consider the exchange-traded fund (ETF) that tracks the NZX MidCap Index and trades under the symbol (MDZ). This is a basket of up to forty stocks led by weightings to Tower Limited (TWR), Infratil Limited (IFT), Ryman Healthcare (RYM) and the Warehouse Group (WHS). These four companies comprise 33% of the total weightings in the basket.

Another idea is to target New Zealand's tourism industry which will benefit when the New Zealand dollar inevitably weakens. Probably the easiest way for foreign investors to play tourist arrivals is via Auckland International Airport (AIA) which handles 70% of all international passengers. The shares yield 4% but trade at an estimated PE of over 23 times. A smaller and less liquid company that benefits from tourism is (not surprisingly) Tourism Holdings. New Zealand tourism should also benefit from holding the 2011 Rugby World Cup.

Despite its small size, New Zealand should not be overlooked particularly when its currency goes the other way and can get very cheap. Keep your powder dry for now and keep a watchful eye on the kiwi.

Indonesia

Jumpstart for Jakarta

Secretary of State Condoleeza Rice's visit to Indonesia this week is hopefully the start of a much closer and broader relationship. This would be great news for Indonesia and America, the Asia-Pacific region and global investors.

The headlines will of course focus on global terrorism and the pivotal role Indonesia plays as the world's largest Muslim nation, the vast majority more moderate and secular than Islamic extremists. Fair enough. For this reason alone Democratic Indonesia warrants America's greatest attention which has been sorely lacking. If we win in Iraq and lose ground in Indonesia, are we really better off?

A second great reason to be more fully engaged with Indonesia is trade and investment. It is a triple play of fostering higher economic growth and incomes in Indonesia, jobs and growth for America and maintaining America's influence in the region which is being undercut by powerful Chinese economic diplomacy. In fact, we need to pay more attention to Indonesia than the Chinese do.

Indonesia's President Yudhoyono, a combination of General, intellectual and bureaucrat, has made real progress in fostering market reforms. Many would categorize Indonesia as a relatively poor country but I beg to differ. I have toured Indonesia from *tip to tip and it is a country with many assets and great promise. Rich in natural resources, a talented and young population, strategically positioned to benefit from Asian growth, a size three times the that of Texas and the world's fourth largest population. As a relatively young democracy and developing economy it lacks an important ingredient for economic growth: capital and a fiscal system to allocate it wisely.*

Let's focus on just one important Indonesia asset that could dramatically jumpstart its economy and stock market while unleashing resources for badly needed education health and infrastructure. This asset is oil and natural gas and Indonesian energy production is far below its potential.

The way that oil production has been handled over the past few years is worse than a blunder and is close to a crime. Indonesia has 10 billion barrels of proven and potential oil reserves and 180 trillion cubic feet of proven and potential reserves. Nevertheless, Indonesia, Asia's only member of OPEC, became a net importer of oil in 2004.

Help is on the way. After five years of tough negotiations, Exxon Mobil and Pertamina will sign a joint-operating agreement this week

Exxon Mobil has operated in Indonesia for a century and invested $17 billion in the country, agreed to explore the dormant Cepu area years ago and by using advanced technology, found proven oil reserves of 600 million barrels and 1.7 trillion cubic feet of gas. Prepared to invest $3 billion to develop the project, it has been waiting for two years to move forward as Indonesia's state-owned energy company Pertamina waited for a better deal. Meanwhile, Indonesia's oil production levels have fallen to less than 900,000 barrels a day!

At peak production, Cepu would provide the GOI about $2 million per day in revenues, add 180,000 barrels a day in daily production and eliminate gas shortages in East Java. There are other projects that could be moved forward and in total could lead to baking an economic pie that could help lift all of the Indonesian people. Moving ahead with these projects would jumpstart the economy and bolster the confidence of foreign investors and capital markets. This is certainly a better option than sharply raising interest rates that choke economic growth and makes badly needed capital even more expensive.

The Indonesian stock market has been one of Asia's best this year up 14.2%. Markets should respond favorably to this deal and I suggest aggressive investors take a look at the closed-end Indonesian Fund (IF) as the best vehicle to invest in Indonesia. It is *managed by Credit Suisse Asset Management and trades at a premium of 7.7% to net asset value with a price of $6.87.*

Although this joint venture will help Indonesia once the oil starts flowing in 2008, it is important that America not just be seen as backing big oil and mining interests. We need a bottom up strategy that gets into fabric of Indonesia village by village. Indonesians need clean water, nutrition, power, consumer products, autos, consumer financing and much more. There is no reason American businesses cannot provide them.

Indonesia has taken the brave step of opening its financial services sector to majority investment by international investors; let's also open up other areas such as infrastructure and power. The most important reform to make Indonesia more attractive to international capital is to set up a transparent and clear approval process to cut out red tape and corruption. Then reinvigorate a previously announced plan to privatize some of Indonesia's 145 largest state-owned companies to increase their profitability and raise more government revenue. Finally, why not follow ten other countries by putting in place a flat tax to rein in bureaucracy, stymie corruption and stimulate growth and productivity.

America needs to be seen as an active and close friend of Indonesia as it continues on the track of democracy, prosperity and progress.

Indonesia Rising

In the beginning of the year, all eyes were on Japan but the Nikkei 225 has been a major disappointment down 6% so far this year. Meanwhile China has done well and Indonesia is the Asia-Pacific region's best market this year up 27% this year. This is despite another tsunami and concerns about bird flu.

Americans, in particular, seem to miss the story of this 3,200 mile archipelago and third largest democracy in the world

The key to a strong Indonesian economy is more trade and investment. It offers a triple play of fostering higher economic growth and incomes in Indonesia, jobs and growth for America and maintaining America's influence in the region which is being undercut by powerful Chinese economic diplomacy. In fact, we need to pay more attention to this Muslim nation with a secular democracy than the Chinese do.

Indonesia's President Yudhoyono, a combination of General, intellectual and bureaucrat, has made real progress in fostering market reforms. Many would categorize

Indonesia as a relatively poor country but I beg to differ. I have toured Indonesia from tip to tip and it is a country with many assets and great promise. Rich in natural resources, a talented and young population, strategically positioned to benefit from Asian growth, a size three times the that of Texas and the world's fourth largest population. As a relatively young democracy and developing economy it lacks an important ingredient for economic growth: capital and a financial system to allocate it efficiently.

Lower interest rates, strong consumer spending has led to real economic growth rate of 6%. The realization that Indonesia is taking steps to better mange its natural resources has also caught the eyes of global investors. Indonesia has 10 billion barrels of proven and potential oil reserves and 180 trillion cubic feet of proven and potential reserves. After five years of tough negotiations, Exxon Mobil and Pertamina finally inked an agreement earlier this year. This should help Indonesia, a member of OPEC, to ramp up production and move towards being a net exporter of energy.

Exxon Mobil has operated in Indonesia for a century and invested $17 billion in the country, agreed to explore the dormant Cepu area years ago and by using advanced technology, found proven oil reserves of 600 million barrels and 1.7 trillion cubic feet of gas. At peak production, Cepu would provide the GOI about $2 million per day in revenues, add 180,000 barrels a day in daily production and eliminate gas shortages in East Java.

Investors have to also keep a close eye on Indonesian politics and the election cycle. While fuel subsidies were cut back sharply reducing pressure on the country's budget and currency, other reforms have been pulled back. The reason is that President Yudhoyono party has only a 10% of parliamentary seats and needs to have the cooperation of other coalition partners to keep power. Indonesia has taken the brave step of opening its financial services sector to majority investment by international investors but it also needs to open up other areas such as infrastructure and power.

The most important reform to make Indonesia more attractive to international capital is to set up a transparent and clear approval process to cut out red tape and corruption. Then reinvigorate a previously announced plan to privatize some of Indonesia's 145 largest state-owned companies to increase their profitability and raise more government revenue.

Finally, why not follow ten other countries by putting in place a flat tax to rein in bureaucracy, stymie corruption and stimulate growth and productivity
The Indonesian stock market has been one of Asia's best this year up 27%. Investors should take a look at the closed-end Indonesian Fund (IF) as the best vehicle to invest

in Indonesia. It is managed by Credit Suisse Asset Management and trades at a premium of 7.7% to net asset value with a price of $6.87.

Philippines

Two Hot Markets

At the beginning of the year, few would have predicted that the best performing stock markets in the Asia-Pacific region would be the Philippines and Indonesia.

The Jakarta Stock Price Index is up 44% year to date and the Philippine Stock Exchange Composite Index is up 32% while the Japanese market is flat as a pancake. While both countries have democratic governments, are sprawling archipelagos and need tremendous amounts of capital, each has its own specific strengths and economic strategies. Unless they attract capital flows to build badly needed infrastructure, sustained economic growth and robust stock market returns are unlikely. And without 7-8% economic growth rates unemployment of their youthful populations will become a political issue leading to more business uncertainty and a slowing of market reforms.

Many would categorize Indonesia and the Philippines as relatively poor countries but I beg to differ. I have led missions to both countries from tip to tip and they have many assets and great promise. Indonesia is rich in natural resources, is strategically positioned to benefit from Asian trade and economic growth, and has a very young population which is the fourth largest in the world. The Philippines strengths are its talented English speaking population giving it the potential to develop into a dynamic regional services hub.

Unfortunately, both countries need massive amounts of foreign investment to meet huge infrastructure needs in the areas of water, power, telecommunications, roads, ports and airports. This infrastructure is like a healthy circulatory system in the human body. Without it, blood and oxygen will be constricted and severe problems are inevitable. Despite the obvious need for this infrastructure capital, not enough is being done to attack the challenges that repel it such as bureaucratic red tape, corruption, lackluster returns relative to risk and legal uncertainties.

But marginal fiscal improvements in both Indonesia and the Philippines have jumpstarted both economies leading to more investment and strong stock markets.

Indonesia's President Yudhoyono, a combination of General, intellectual and bureaucrat, has made some progress in fostering market reforms most notably cutting fuel subsidies. Lower interest rates and strong consumer spending has led to an economic growth rate of 6-7%. The realization that Indonesia is taking steps to better mange its natural resources has also caught the eyes of global investors. After five years of tough negotiations, Exxon Mobil and the state oil company Pertamina finally inked an agreement earlier this year. This should help Indonesia, a member of OPEC, to ramp up production and move towards being a net exporter of energy. In addition, China's Huadian Corporation recently announced plans to build a $2 billion power plant in South Sumatra and the government at a well publicized conference this month opened to foreign investors 110 infrastructure projects valued at $16.5 billion.

Philippine's President Gloria Macapagal has weathered a coup attempt prompted in part by her administration's pushing through a tax bill which increased tax collections to lessen dependence on foreign borrowing. This has led to lower interest rates, a stronger peso and higher consumer spending and economic growth. Still the need to lessen congestion in Manila and stem the exodus of talented Filipinos is palpable. Better infrastructure in Manila and other parts of the Philippines will go a long way to solve these two pressing problems.

With high consumer demand for these infrastructure services as well as political pressure to deliver the goods, investors could do well by investing in companies that address these pressing needs.

For the Philippines, Philippine Long Distance better known as PLDT (PHI), is the Goliath in the Philippine stock market, accounting for a large chunk of its entire market cap. Think of it as a proxy for a market that doesn't have an exchange traded fund. And with the company trading at a P/E of 11.5, you're buying it at a 30% discount to its counterpart in nearby Indonesia.

For Indonesia, the long wait for expensive landline telephone services has spurred the rapid growth of cellular services. INDOSAT is the country's second largest cellular operator and while earnings comparisons this year have been disappointing, more than 70% of total revenue is coming from cellular operations. In 2002, the Government of Indonesia wisely divested 41% of its shares to a company controlled by Singapore Technologies Telemedia. The stock is listed on the Indonesia, Singapore and New York Stock Exchange.

The Indonesia Fund (IF) was a holding we had in the Asian Portfolio until we sold it after about a 40% gain year to date. Aggressive investors might still garner some gains but should use caution and a stop loss.

These markets tend to be a bit volatile so it is wise not to get carried away. Have some risk management tools in place such as a 10% trailing stop loss order in order to lock in gains. Both Indonesia and the Philippines still have some upside but the best time to score large gains is when investors are not showing the slightest interest in these markets.

Vietnam

Merrill Bullish on Vietnam

Because of its thinly traded market and lack of investment options, global investors often overlook Vietnam's potential. Not Merrill Lynch.

Merrill Lynch has acquired a coveted "trading code" needed to buy and sell shares directly on Vietnam's small but growing stock market. Merrill Lynch obtained the right to directly hold Vietnamese shares last week, six months after Spencer White, the bank's chief regional strategist, called Vietnamese stocks a "10-year buy".

Vietnam is slightly larger than New Mexico in size but has a population of 85 million half of whom are under the age of 25 years. Vietnam's economic growth rate of 8% is close to that of China and its manufacturing capability has a long way to go representing just 11% of GDP. Wage rates are lower than its neighboring competitors and the service side of the economy is thriving.

I am no fan of the Communist Party of Vietnam but market liberalization and reform is sporadically moving ahead. It is also gradually becoming integrated into the global economy. On May 31st, Vietnam signed a bilateral agreement with the U.S. to accede to the World Trade Organization (WTO) by the end of the year. This was followed by the U.S. Senate's decision to award Permanent Normal Trading Relations (PNTR) status to Vietnam on July 31st—eleven years after diplomatic ties between the two nations were re-established. Vietnam's recent growth has been driven primarily by exports which were up 26% during the first half of this year. Leading the charge is textile and garment manufacturing, oil and mining, agriculture and food processing.

Vietnam has a tiny but growing stock market. With 48 members, 47 listed companies, and one domestic fund, the Vietnam Stock Exchange (VSE) has a current *market capitalization of $3 billion. In early 2005, it had a market cap of only $200 million. There were 12 IPOs in the first half of this year but incredibly two companies still account for half of the market's capitalization.*

This thin market is volatile and after rising almost 70% in the first part of the year has lost about 30% of its value during the past 12 weeks. Not for the faint of heart. Foreign ownership in listed securities is permitted, but it is capped at 49% for most companies and only 30% for banks.

Still, for long-term, far-sighted investors, the attractions are clear. the young literate workforce that is consumer oriented, a very under developed banking system that is on the cusp of major change, rising foreign direct investment, cost advantages in growing its manufacturing sector, strong export growth, and has huge upside potential as a tourist destination. It's market also offers attractive valuations which according to Merrill Lynch with PE multiples of 8x-10x, EPS growth of 20 per cent-40 per cent and dividend yields range from 3 per cent to 10 per cent.

There is always the risk that reform efforts will falter and corruption and the bureaucratic red tape will continue to challenge even the most persistent and committed company entering the Vietnam market. The country's bureaucracy is as labyrinthine as ever and it has a opaque legal system with separate laws for foreign and domestic investors. Foreign invest investments in companies is capped at 49% and 30% for banks.

There are only a few direct plays for investors—the Vietnam Opportunity Fund (VOF) listed on the London Stock Exchange. It is trading at $2.37 down from a high of $2.62 earlier this year. Another option is the Dublin-listed Vietnam Growth Fund.

Another option is a neighboring country with a somewhat lower risk profile, similar growth potential and more developed market—Indonesia. It is also the world's third largest democracy which is a big advantage over Vietnam's Communist government. The Indonesia Fund (IF) is a closed-end fund that is currently in Chartwell's Asian Opportunity portfolio. It is up 28% over the past year and its annualized total return through over the past three years through July is an eye catching 40.4%. You can build a small position at current price of $8.48 since the premium to the funds net asset value is only 3.8%, substantially below the norm.

Treat any portfolio allocation to Vietnam or Indonesia as if you were investing in an emerging market venture capital fund. It is a speculative position and will take time to develop. The potential payoff makes it worth the risk in my book.

Europe & Canada

Switzerland

The Swiss Pack a Punch

Do you think of Switzerland as a quaint staid tourist country with great chocolate and fine watches? Or as another example of "Old Europe" with high taxes and big government which stifles economic growth? Think again.

For starters, Switzerland is home to four of the largest five firms in Europe in terms of market capitalization: UBS, Nestle, Novartis, and Roche. It also has the highest per capita income in the world.

While only 137 miles by 216 miles in size with a population of 7.2 million, Switzerland packs a punch and is a financial and multinational powerhouse. Let's take a quick look at the asset side of Switzerland's balance sheet.

It has a strong currency backed by ample gold reserves, fiscal discipline, trade surplus and very little foreign debt. Outward looking, Switzerland has 40% of its GDP attributed to exports. Switzerland represents the third largest financial center in the world after New York and London. It is also home to world-beating pharmaceutical, engineering and food companies

Switzerland enjoys a stable government, vibrant democracy and a reputation as an asset haven in times of stress. The Swiss have had a functioning democracy for 500 years and actually has a fairly weak central government with a legislature that meets for only two weeks four times a year. Voters actually defeated a referendum which would have given them a shorter workweek and longer vacations. All men between the ages of 20 and 42 are required to engage in military training each summer resulting in an army of 625,000. Swiss guards have protected the Vatican since 1506.

Sounds pretty good—now why and how should Switzerland become part of your portfolio?

Large blue chip global companies are back in favor due to attractive price-to-value valuations, entrenched brand names, dominant market shares, proven management teams, solid free cash flows and double digit growth potential. What better way to play this trend than with Swiss quality, value and growth.

The iShares Switzerland ETF (EWL) is a wonderful way to gain exposure to Switzerland's leading multinationals and has an expense ration of only 0.59%. My favorite stock pick is Nestle (NSRGY) which has all of the above attributes plus a share buyback program and a rising dividend. ABB is another favorite and has been on a tear winning power and automation technology contacts all over the world. Its order rate is up 15% so far this year but its stock price (ABB) is getting a bit rich at $8.65. Wait for it to fall back through $8 before building a position.

You can't go wrong with Swiss quality if the price is right.

Germany

Germany's Upside

Why was former Chancellor Gerhard Schroeder smiling broadly in all those pictures with Chancellor Angela Merkel? He knows just how tough it is going to be to turn the German supertanker around with an unwieldy left-right coalition at the controls.

Americans should thank heaven each morning that they have only Democrats and Republicans to worry about. Multi-party coalition governments are infinitely more difficult to manage. Consider this: the agreement between Germany's ruling coalition is 190 pages long.

Making everything more difficult is the contradictory policies of the new government. The coalition's stated primary goal is to create jobs and bring the 11% unemployment rate down but it also plans on raising taxes to reduce the budget deficit which has missed the European Union's fiscal rules for the fourth straight year. In addition, plans to reduce Germany's corporate tax rate and radical labor reforms have already been put off to 2008.

The gateway to growth is in the hands of the German consumer who is by all accounts "conservative". Polls show that most have very low expectations of the incoming government. 61% believe that German's economic situation will be worse four years from now and only 16% believe that Chancellor Merkel can sharply decrease the unemployment rate. No wonder consumer spending has decreased three quarters in a row.

Germans know that they need to make some significant changes but are resistant to dismantle the expensive social net and inflexible labor regulations that hamper German growth. The key issue is the former East Germany. Germany has poured $1.5 trillion into the region and unemployment is still about 19%. Instead of taking advantage of its lower wage structure, German unions rushed to unionize East German workers that did not have the training, skills or mindset commensurate with their jump in wages.

The brightest spot for Germany has been exports of industrial goods with especially strong exports to China. But this is changing as China makes more of these capital goods itself. In the last 12 months, Chinese exports to Germany have risen 40% while German exports to China have risen a paltry 2%. Germans have a high savings rate of 11% of income and GDP growth has averaged only 0.5% during the last three years.

I have painted a rather bleak picture so why have I recommended a modest allocation to the German iShare since May 2005?

The first reason is very low expectations. Any improvements, even marginal, will have a positive affect on markets. Secondly, the overall market is not expensive at about 14 times earnings. Thirdly, the German companies that dominate the holdings of the Germany iShare are world-class multinationals and are more tied to booming Asia than to the slow growth German economy. Large German multinationals are shedding high cost and inflexible German workers. Siemens, Deutsche Telecom, Allianz, Deutsche Bank, DaimlerChrysler, Bayer and BASF account for 50% of the holdings of the Germany iShare (EWG).

Furthermore, with the Euro down (check year end number) % this year and at a two year low against the U.S. Dollar, the world's largest exporter is picking up some steam. The top line numbers from leading German industrial companies are rolling in with impressive numbers for an almost zero growth economy. Siemens quarterly sales rose 13%—the fastest since 2003. BMW's sales rose by 11% in the third quarter although high raw material costs and pricing pressure resulted in weak net profits. A bright spot is Asia where BMW expects to sell 150,000 cars per year by 2008.

Overall, German exports are up for the third straight month and sales to countries outside of the European Union rose 18% annually from a year earlier. Clearly the Germans are good at making stuff and selling it to the world and the weaker Euro is helping spur growth. Germany's DAX stock index is taking notice and was up % in 2005.

The German economy is a huge restructuring play that will take many years to bear fruit so investors should go with large German multinationals such as ABB and Siemens that are not waiting for the politicians to tell them what to do. They are searching the globe for opportunities and winning big contracts and profits for shareholders.

Netherlands

Dutch Treats and Flemish Flavor

In the Dutch golden age during the 17th century, Dutch trading, science and art dominated the world scene. It still packs a global punch and is often overlooked by investors.

About twice the size of New Jersey with a population of 16.5 million, the Kingdom of the Netherlands is a prosperous and open economy with a bent towards trading with the world. The top multinationals based in the Netherlands accounted for a combined revenue of $822 billion of revenue in 2005.

It is easy to tap into in this global corporate vigor through the Netherlands iShare (EWN) that contains a basket of 27 Dutch companies. The global financial services firm ING accounts for 18% of the basket. ING has a dominant position in growing Asian markets such as China, India and Thailand and its direct bank now has 15 million customers worldwide. 50% of its profits come from insurance operations and since European and American markets are rather mature, it's strategy is to continue to diversify geographically and move into higher growth areas such as retirement services. ING is a low cost provider resulting in an ROE in 2005 of 24% though the relatively high debt load is a concern.

The next four highest weighted companies in this ETF are all top quality: ABN Amro, Phillips Electronics, Unilever and Aegon. In terms of sectors, diversified financials account for 18% of the basket, food, beverage and tobacco is 13%, banks, 13% and consumer durables 10%.

The Netherlands stock market is undervalued with its AEX index trading at a price earnings ratio of 12 times earnings.

Belgium, which broke away from the Netherlands in 1830, also presents investors with solid value. King Albert II reigns over this industrious nation with Dutch— speaking Flemings in the north and French-speaking Walloons in the south. Belgium sits at the crossroads of Europe and is home to both NATO and the European Union.

The Belgium ETF (EWK) contains 23 companies with the insurance and banking behemoth Fortis leading the way with 23% of the basket. The stock is 14% off its 52 week high and in the first quarter of 2006 its net profits before divestments was up 25%. Financials and banks make up more than 50% the holdings of the Belgium ETF with materials, food and telecom companies adding an additional 22%.

The Belgium stock market is undervalued trading at 1.9 times book with a forward price earnings ratio of 12. It enjoys low interest rates and according to data from EmergingPortfolio.com, global money managers have increased their Belgium weightings in the most recent month.

Add both Netherlands (EWN) and Belgium (EWK) to your global ETF portfolios to balance more aggressive allocations to emerging market countries.

Sweden

Sweden's Time to Choose

There are many who scoff that politics should have much to do with investing. When selecting ETFs for Chartwell's portfolios, I look at several factors such as fundamentals of companies in the ETF basket, capital flows, technical factors, macro indicators, currencies and so on. But the direction of market reforms which is what politics is all about sometimes rises to the top. Think of the Reagan led Republican sweep in 1980 and the significant tax cuts and market reforms in Ireland and Australia which preceded their strong economic growth and sustained bull markets.

Sweden is just such a case with a key election on September 17th. For 65 of the last 74 years and the last 12 years, the center-left Social Democrats have been in control but the center-right opposition led by Mr. Fredrik Reinfeldt is mounting an effective campaign for change. The issues of deregulation, tax cuts, privatization and job creation are leading his reform agenda.

In January, Ericsson's CEO Carl-Henric Svenberg announced his support for change and other key Swedish industrialists have followed suit. Sweden's public sector accounts for 30% of its total workforce (15% in US and EU) and the state oversees 57 businesses with a market value of $70 billion while employing 200,000 people. There was some deregulation of the telecom, auto and banking sectors in the 1990s which led to good growth but this time the impact and stakes could be much higher.

The Kingdom of Sweden, with a population of 9 million and area exceeding that of California, has many attributes which investors should appreciate. King Carl Gustav (no relation) has reigned since 1973 over a well educated citizenry. It is blessed with ample natural resources like iron ore, copper, gold, timber, lead, zinc and hydro power but 70% of its economy is driven by services. Sweden's per capita GDP is $30,000 and it has a balanced budget surplus, current account surplus, opted out of euro in 2003 and a vigilant central bank (Riksbank) which is targeting an inflation rate of 2%. Sweden's stockmarket is also reasonably priced at 12.2 times earnings.

We have had the Swedish ETF (EWD) in some portfolios for some time with positive results. This year it is up 14% and over the last 12 months 19%. Ericsson accounts for 21% of the basket with quality companies like Svenska, Sandvik, Volvo and Atlas Copco all top ten holdings that readers might be familiar with. Capital good, technology and banking each contribute about 20% of sector exposure.

Below is a point and figure chart for (EWD) and some commentary provided by Don Smith, President of go2mypv.com.

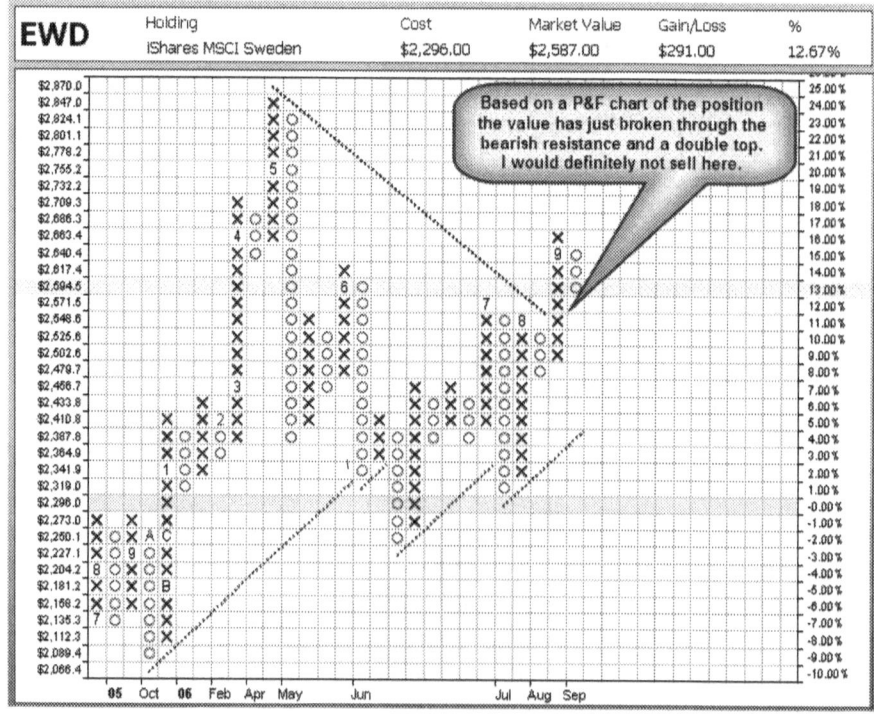

I also recommend some exposure to the Swedish Krona which I think will marginally outperform the Euro. Rydex has an ETF (FXS) which tracks the Krona.

The ruling Social Democrats led by Prime Minister Goran Persson are fighting back furiously raising fears of radical change and attacking venture capitalists for calling for change at companies like Volvo. Given Mr. Reinfeldt's assurances of moving smartly and incrementally and his strong and broad support amongst the business community, his party will be victorious.

Don't wait until the election later this week, act now.

Canada

Canada Plays China Card

Trade friction and energy leverage has led to an unprecedented Canadian policy of "speak loudly and carry a big piece of lumber" policy towards the United States.

The long running dispute over American tariffs on Canadian lumber escalated to the point last week that Canadian Prime Minister Paul Martin indirectly linked settlement with continued U.S. access to Canadian energy supplies. Meanwhile, Canadian Natural Resources Minister John McCallum was off to China to meet with Chinese oil, mining and forestry officials.

This is serious business. Part of the 1994 NAFTA Free Trade Agreement guaranteed that Canada would remain the favored supplier to the U.S. It might surprise you to learn that Canada supplies 17% of U.S. oil imports, 16% of our natural gas and nearly all of our hydroelectric power. The Canadian government owns the vast majority of the country's energy resources and Canada exports more than 1.5 million barrels a day to America representing 8% of U.S. consumption.

Meanwhile, China's aggressive moves in Canada's energy sector are raising eyebrows in Washington. Chinese government has earmarked $100 billion for overseas acquisitions of oil and gas. The Chinese are going on a buying spree investing in Canadian energy companies and recently plunked down $2 billion to build a thousand mile pipeline from Alberta tar sands to port on the west coast and onward to Beijing and Shanghai. While the oil reserve numbers for Saudi Arabia are under scrutiny, Canada has recoverable reserves of roughly 175 million barrels. Much of it is in oil sand that is *processed profitably at oil prices of $20 or higher and T. Boone Pickens thinks that Canada's oil sand production could reach 6 million barrels a day*

There are now about 1 million ethnic Chinese residing in Canada and China is now Canada's second largest trading partner. Last month, Chinese President Hu Jintao visited Canada and declared that the two countries had upgraded their relations to a "strategic partnership".

This Chinese-Canadian power play puts America in real jam. You could write a book about the long simmering lumber dispute but a Nafta panel recently ordered the U.S. to return $5 billion of collected tariffs to Canadian lumber companies. Relations with Canada were also weakened earlier this year when Canada announced that it would not contribute to the American-led missile defense program even though 90% of Canadian citizens live within 100 mile of the border between the two countries and Americans purchase 85% of total Canadian exports.

What's going on? Part of the answer is that the vast majority of Canadians oppose the policies of the Bush Administration. The issue is sensitive in many areas across Canada that are highly dependent on the lumber industry and Mr. Martin and his party are preparing for national elections expected early next year. It is always a vote getter to poke a stick in the eye of the elephant to the south.

While Canadian-American relations have seen better days, the energy boom has certainly been beneficial to investors in Canadian markets. The Canada iShare (EWC) tracks the MSCI Canada Index that has 40% exposure to Canada's energy and materials sector. While the S&P index is up only 3%, the Canada iShare is up 16.6% year to date and 28.8% over the past twelve months.

Speaking of timber, it is smart to have some timber exposure in your portfolio and I have had timber REIT Plum Creek Timber (PCL) in our core portfolio for over two years. Here is why I like it. First, timber is a great inflation hedge and over the past 100 years has risen 3% above the average annual inflation rate. Secondly, timber is not correlated to stocks or bonds and thus is a great "shock absorber" to cushion your portfolio when shares are declining. During the 1970s bear market, timber rose in value while stocks went down. Thirdly, from 1973-2000 timber yielded an average annual return of 15%. Last but not least, timber valuations are attractive after some declines during 2000-2002 especially relative to real estate prices. During 2004 Plum Creek was up 23% and this year it has traded between $34 and $39 finishing last week just over $35 with an attractive dividend yield of 4.3%.

It behooves the U.S. to negotiate a settlement to the lumber dispute as soon as possible and lock up Canadian energy sources before the Chinese get the jump on us. Investors can't do much about improving Canadian-American relations but they can improve their portfolios by adding exposure to timber as well as to Canada as both an energy and China play.

Latin America

Chile

Hot Chile

With Chile hosting this years APEC meeting, it seems appropriate to take a look at this economic star of Latin America.

Chile is about two times the size of Montana and has an incredible coastline of 2,650 miles. While only 3% of its land is arable, it has an amazing variety of climates and rich agricultural production. It gained its independence from Spain in 1810 and has 16 million citizens of which 90% are Catholic.

The Chile story is somewhat similar to Ireland before its economic takeoff. From 1978 to 1988, per capita income increased only $100 to reach $1,510.

Next, both a military government followed by democratically elected governments initiated market reforms and opened up the economy. Exports and foreign investment took off and debt levels came down. Foreign investors in Chile are treated the same as Chilean investors.

From 1991-1998 economic growth increased an average of 8% and per capita income on a purchasing power basis has grown to $10,700. Since then growth has moderated to a 4-5% range but public Chilean total public and foreign debt at 50% of GDP is very low relative to other Latin countries.

Trade is very important to Chile with exports accounting for 25% of GDP. It is rich in natural resources (copper, timber, fruit and fish) and has been busy signing free trade agreements. A Free Trade Agreement (FTA) with the US took effect in January 2004 and now 90% of Chile's exports to the US enter duty free. After a similar trade pact with South Korea last year, exports rose 50%.

Current President Ricardo Lagos Escobar is under pressure to improve economic growth rates and bring down the stubbornly high 8% unemployment rate. On the positive side, inflation and interest rates are low at 2-3%. Chile has demonstrated fiscal discipline and enjoys both a trade surplus and a budget surplus.

There are no country-specific ETF's for Chile but there is the Chile Fund (CH) which is a closed-end fund managed by Credit Suisse Asset Management. It is up 53% over the past year, trades at a 7.7% discount to its net asset value and sports a 4.6% yield. Keep in mind that 19% of the fund is invested in just one copper company Empresas Copec S.A. and the annual fee is high at 1.80%.

Another alternative would be the iShares Latin America 40 (ILF) which invests in Mexico, Brazil, Chile and Argentina. It is up an eye opening 67% over the past twelve months with an annual fee of only 0.55%. Currently, 49% of this exchange-traded fund is invested in Brazil, 38% in Mexico, 10% in Chile and 3% in Argentina.

Interested investors might also consider the ADR for Banco Santander (SAN) which is an excellent bank and a good proxy for the overall economy. It is up 42% over the past year and up 11% so far this year. Banco Santander is one of the 30 companies in the Chartwell Global 30 Index which is an alternative to the Dow Jones Industrial Average.

Brazil

Brazil's Stronger Balance Sheet

Brazil's booming stock market has caught foreign investor's attention but the question still lurks in the background like an uninvited guest—is this just another leg in the typical boom and bust cycle?

For the answer, take a look at Brazil's improving balance sheet. While America piles on the debt, Brazil is going the other way. It decided last December to pay off its remaining $15.5 billion debt with the International Monetary Fund (that must be a relief!) and announced just last week that it will retire all of its remaining $6.6 billion worth of Brady bonds issued during the early 1990's financial crisis

Where is the money coming from? Brazil recorded trade surpluses in 2004 and 2005 with exports for the last twelve months hitting a record $120 billion. Exports of oil, soybeans, copper, steel, autos, sugar and coffee are surging even in the face of a strengthening currency. The Brazilian real is up 52% against the US dollar since May

2004 and up 22% during 2005. Brazil is almost energy independent and foreign exchange reserves are now $58 billion even after paying off the nettlesome IMF debt.

Behind all these positive numbers are substantial reforms begun by President Cardosa and continued by Luiz Inacio "Lula" da Silva. Payroll taxes and corporate taxes have been cut, the tax system simplified and last week Brazil announced that it would eliminate the income tax for foreigners that purchase public debt. Brazil's strong currency will likely also lead to a loosening of foreign exchange restrictions.

A cynical friend of mine often comments that successful political leaders need to ignore their strongest supporters if they are to achieve real reform. If so, Lula is a good example since most expected him to reverse market reforms after taking power in 2002 while in fact he deepened them. Up for re-election in October, Lula has nevertheless delivered higher living standards and restored national pride. With 187 million people and an area only slightly smaller than the United States, this leading South American economic power together with Chile and Colombia are changing attitudes toward the region as a whole.

What's the best way to bet on Brazil's momentum and improving balance sheet. I had been recommending the Brazil iShare (EWZ) which is up 27% this year and 72% in the last 12 months. In June of last year I switched to the S&P Latin America 40 iShare (ILO) that gives you broader exposure with 50% exposure to Brazil, 38% to Mexico, 9% to Chile and 3% to Argentina. This ETF is up 18% this year and 69% over the last year.

One ADR to take a look at is wireless provider that has been on a tear America Movil (AMX) and a safer option is Colgate Palmolive which derives roughly 20% of its sales from Latin American markets.

How important is the October election to Brazil? Even with all the economic growth, lower debt, lower taxes, booming exports and strong currency, public sector debt is still 51% of GDP so continued progress is essential. Like the old saw goes, even if you are on the right track, if you're not moving you could get run over.

Specialty ETFs

Magnificent Gold

Last week during his tour of Kyoto Japan, President Bush visited the Golden Pavilion (Kinkakuji) and described it as "magnificent". He was probably referring to the 1398 Japanese architecture but may just as well have been referring to gold prices which are at an 18-year high. Gold has been a magnificent investment and still has considerable upside.

It is a rare portfolio that I build for a client that does not have some allocation to gold and other precious metals. There are three basic reasons why investors should still consider adding it to their portfolio.

First, gold prices are not normally correlated to other asset class prices. It therefore serves as a buffer or shock absorber to the value of a portfolio when other assets classes are out of favor.

Secondly, there are supply and demand factors. Central banks have been net sellers of gold over the past twenty years. Gold accounts for about 9% of the $4.4 trillion in world central bank foreign exchange and gold reserves, down from 15% in early 2000.

But some central banks are now going the other way. For example, the Russian central bank wants to increase gold's share of its reserves from 5% to 10%.

Jewelry demand for gold is also picking up especially in China and India. Global investors are also using gold as a hedge for a global recession and potential decline in value of the U.S. dollar or the Euro.

On the supply side, production of gold has been relatively flat for the last 5-7 years and does not appear to be turning around due to maturing mines and higher extraction costs.

The third reason to have some gold exposure in your portfolio is that it serves as disaster insurance from unforeseen but potentially devastating events such as widespread terrorism or severe economic or political upheaval.

Many gold bugs insist that the only true gold exposure is through gold coins. An easier way to gain instant gold exposure is through the iShares COMEX Gold Trust ETF (IAU) that is up 15.3% so far this year. Another option is investing through the iShares South Africa ETF (EZA) which has considerable exposure to the gold and mining industry and is up 15.9% this year.

Don't come down with gold fever. A 5-10% allocation to your core conservative portfolio should get the job done. Expect some lusterless years as well as some magnificent returns and restful nights knowing you have some gold under the pillow.

Load Silver ETF Bullet

William Jennings Bryan's "Cross of Gold" speech on July 9, 1896 electrified the Democratic National Convention giving the 36 year old the inside track on capturing the presidential nomination.

The speech addressed the issue of monetary policy and the debate over backing the dollar with gold and silver rather than just gold which was deemed overly restrictive and unfair to working people and farmers. It ended with this memorable sentence:

"You shall not press down upon the brow of labor this crown of thorns; you shall not crucify mankind upon a cross of gold."

Gold ETFs have attracted huge inflows by investors seeking a hedge on inflation, protection against global fiscal imbalances, a weak dollar and the search for positions that hopefully will not be closely correlated to global equities.

It's time to take a closer look at silver and the silver ETF which has come back sharply to a price under its launch price earlier this year.

Silver has long been the neglected orphan of the precious metals markets. Investor sentiment towards silver has been depressed by the perception the demand for silver in film and paper for photo imaging falling sharply due to the rise of digital technology. But photography only accounts for about 8% of total demand for silver.

Actually, silver has some of the best-looking supply and demand fundamentals in the metals markets. The demand for silver is rising fast, due to both increasing demand for the raw material for the manufacture of jewelry and silverware, and because it has so many industrial applications.

It is, for example, one of the best electrical conductors of all the metals. "Every time a homeowner turns on a microwave oven, dishwasher, clothes washer or television set, the action activates a switch with silver contacts", says the Silver Institute.

However, the real case for investing in silver lies on the supply side because silver really is quite rare. There are only 23 pure silver mines operating around the world and most of the silver supply comes as a by-product from mines mainly engaged in digging for lead, zinc and copper. Furthermore, silver production was flat this year and is expected to be flat again next year.

Mined silver has been less than demand every single year for the last 15 years but this hasn't been a huge problem because the world has been able to fill the gap from inventories and official stockpiles.

However, today the US government stockpile is all but gone and sales from other official sources such as China, Russia and India appear to be declining too. According to research consultant CPM, in 1990 there were around 2.2 billion ounces of silver held in above-ground stocks. Today, there are probably only about 300 million. That's a 50-year low.

The SilverStockReport.com notes that while about 95% of the gold ever mined still exists in above-ground refined form, 95% of the silver ever mined has been consumed by electronics and jewelry. Aside from industrial demand/supply imbalances, silver is once again being viewed by many as a pure metals investing play.

When the Silver ETF (SLV) was launched in on April 21st at a price of $121, I recommended to clients to sit on the sidelines because of the rapid run up in silver price during the SEC registration process. Since then, the silver ETF price has fallen from a high of $152 in early May back to $119 while accumulating $1.2 billion of silver.

With an annual fee of only 0.50%, the silver ETF is the cleanest and easiest way to gain some exposure to silver. Another option is to invest in one or more of the largest silver miners but they are for the most part located in somewhat unstable countries such as Bolivia and Peru. The top six silver miners have a combined market cap of just $8 billion and do not seem particularly cheap to me. The largest silver miner in the world is BHP Billiton (BHP) which I have liked for some tome and now has a market cap larger than Coca-Cola. BHP is also the largest position in the Australian ETF (EWA).

William Jennings Bryan's "Cross of Gold" speech is a classic and investors can benefit from his captivating message 110 year later. Put the silver ETF in your core portfolio with a trailing stop loss of 10%.

Saddle Up on the Commodity Bull

It seems like 2006 will be another profitable year in what I believe is a major commodity bull run that could last for many years. Crude oil prices are still at lofty levels, gold hit its highest level since 1981, silver climbed to a 17-year high and copper and zinc have also reached new record highs. What is driving this trend and what is the best way for the individual investor without inclination to follow the intricacies of these markets?

Higher demand from emerging markets such as China is a major factor. Precious metal prices may also be reacting to speculation that some central banks may diversify away from the U.S. dollar and to precious metals.

The explosion of new commodity investment vehicles and the perception of commodities as an inflation hedge may also be driving demand. Global political uncertainties are also affecting markets. The situation in Iran, the fourth-largest crude producer in the world, is just one of the trouble zones that have markets on edge.

Whether as a way to invest in global growth or a hedge on inflation and political uncertainties, it makes an awful lot of sense to have some exposure to commodities in your global portfolio. Not being correlated to stocks or bonds, they also reduce overall portfolio risk and increase the chances of achieving greater returns.

But deciding on the best vehicle for investing in commodities can be a daunting task. Managed future funds have high minimums, commissions and fees and the use of leverage can lead to unexpected volatility. There are a few simple ways to gain exposure without high costs or betting on one commodity.

First, take a look at AngloAmerican (AAUK), a huge conglomerate and leading natural resources and mining company with significant exposure to commodities. It owns 45% of De Beers, the largest producer and marketer of gem diamonds in the world. It seems logical that rising disposable incomes and wealth in India and China will lead to commensurate higher demand for precious gems in both countries. According to the Diamond Registry in New York, the growth rate in China is about 20% a year compared to 6% in America. De Beers also plans to open outlets in 17 mainland cities as part of a $16 million marketing campaign.

AngloAmerican also accounts for 38% of the global supply of platinum and has exposure to copper nickel and zinc, not to mention significant coal production. Recently there's been a modest pullback in the prices of base metals, primarily from broad profit taking, says Patricia Mohr, vice president of commodities research at Scotiabank. She also notes that crude and natural gas prices have dropped recently because of warmer winter weather in some areas.

Next, consider the first exchange-traded fund (ETF) to track a commodity index, the Deutsche Bank Commodity Index ETF (DBC). It gives investors exposure to a basket of the most liquid and deep commodity markets in the world. The current weightings are: 35%, light, sweet crude oil, 20% heating oil, 12.5% aluminum, 11.25% corn, 11.25% wheat and 10% gold.

Another good option is the country-specific iShares that have sizable exposure to commodity markets such as Australia (ewa), Canada (ewc), and South Africa (eza). The Australia iShare has 28% exposure to the materials and energy sector including an 11% exposure to the largest mining company in the world BHP Billiton (bhp). There are also on the market several ETF gold options and iShares is reportedly seeking SEC approval for an ETF tracking silver prices.

And don't forget coffee, the world's second largest commodity after oil. Asia's, and in particular China's, rising disposable incomes, plus an acquired taste for coffee, could spur consumption leading to explosive demand. If China gets to South Korea's or Taiwan's per capita coffee consumption levels, it could literally purchase total current world coffee production.

Investing on the production side is not for the faint of heart because of hard-to-predict coffee price fluctuations. The most attractive option may be to invest in the retail coffee market which is highly fragmented. Starbucks (sbux) is the global leader, with 10,500 retail outlets of which 3,500 are outside North America.

Starbucks began in Asia with its first store in Japan in 1996 and now has 165 stores in mainland China, 221 in Hong Kong, Taiwan and Macau, 595 in Japan, 64 in Australia and 34 in Singapore. Its global goal is to reach 30,000 outlets with half of them located overseas. China could very well become its second-largest market after America. Don't get carried away with commodities—they're too volatile to be the core of your portfolio, but blending in some of these options will give you diversification.

Graduate to Nanotech ETF

In the movie "The Graduate" is the unforgettable scene at a cocktail party, when a businessman leans over and whispers into young Dustin Hoffman's ear that "plastics" is the next great growth industry. Perhaps today he might have suggested nanotech. I am no scientist and my guess is that you aren't either. So how can we get comfortable with nanotech and, more importantly, invest in it?

First of all, what is nanotech? The word "nano" is Greek for small and a nanometer is really small—one billionth of a meter. Written with nanometer letters, 20 volumes of Forbes archives could fit on the tip of a pin. Nanotechnology cuts across the disciplines of physics, chemistry and biology and deals with working with these molecules and sub-atomic particles to create, control, manipulate and organize them into new structures and new uses. Commercially developing new materials with new properties means big breakthroughs and big bucks. The applications are endless, medicines, energy, agriculture, textiles, and so on. Nanotech also has the potential to crush existing products and technologies.

Ok, I hope you have the picture, this could be big. But what is the smart way for an investor to get a piece of the action? You could try to pick specific nanotech companies but which ones? Your guess is as good as mine. A better approach may be to buy a basket of these stocks with the thinking that most of them won't pan out but a few might hit it big. A good tool for this approach would be the Powershares Nanotech ETF (PXN) which was launched in October, 2005.

This ETF basket contains 26 companies involved in nanotech with 68% of them categorized as small cap growth and 22% as large cap value. The ETF has a composite p/e of 18 and is trading at $17 down from a 52 week high of $20. One of the aspects of Powershares ETFs I like is that they are not market cap weighted so you get a more even distribution in company weightings. In the nanotech ETF, the largest holding is NVE Corp. at 8.6% followed by Nanophase Technologies at 5.4%. Next comes eight companies in the 4% area so an investor gets a nice balanced exposure.

This ETF is of course speculative and you need to think of it a bit like a venture capital fund. Chartwell has built a nice portfolio of similar forward-looking Powershares into a portfolio called the "New Venture" portfolio. In addition to the nanotech ETF, there are allocations to sectors like clean energy (PBW), water resources (PHO) and dynamic pharmaceuticals (PJP).

I hope that nanotech's promise meets the high expectations. At the very least, you will be able to mention casually at a cocktail party that you are a nanotech investor. Impressive, to say the least.

"A Call to Economic Arms"

A Blueprint to Meet
the Challenge from a Rising Asia

Carl T. Delfeld

Chairman
Chartwell America Foundation

President
Chartwell Partners
ChartwellETFAdvisor.com

The San Francisco Money Show, October, 2006

Many say that America is at the pinnacle of its economic power and global influence but the 21st century belongs to Asia. I believe that if we take action for the common good, America's best days are yet to come.

History shows that great countries and civilizations fail due to one or more of three shortcomings: a lack of fiscal discipline, a culture that does not promote openness, scientific innovation or the common good, and a foreign policy not grounded in the national interest and executed at the extremes of isolationism or foreign interventionism.

America has been blessed by geography, ample natural resources and a free form of government that allows it to be strong, secure and independent even as it participates fully in the global marketplace.

But America needs a spurt of creativity and growth that resembles the period in the early 20th century when it first became a dominant player on the global economic stage.

Here is how Charles Morris describes this era in the opening of his book "The Tycoons":

"America was not only the most populous of industrial countries but the richest by any standard.—per capita income, natural resource endowment, industrial production, the value of its farms and factories. It dominated world markets—not just in steel and oil but in wheat and cotton. It ran huge trade surpluses in goods and was gaining preeminence in financial services. Its people were the most mobile, the most productive, the most inventive, and, on average, the best educated....
Attentive European elites were shocked as they came to understand the scale and speed of America's ascendancy"

Of course the American economy is now at a different stage of development and many of the comments about America in the above passage are still apt today.

America is still the fastest-growing of the large industrialized economies. More than 700 of the world's largest 2,000 companies are headquartered in America and we also lead in global entrepreneurship. The vitality of the American economy is highlighted by the fact that only twenty of the current Fortune 100 companies were even around in 1980. Very importantly, we still have the deepest and most liquid capital markets in the world.

While America still leads, the evidence is clear that the world is filling in and other countries are catching up rapidly. To underscore and highlight dramatic changes taking place in global economy—here are some snapshots

- *China now has world's largest FX reserves—over $1 trillion*

- *Emerging market countries account for 83% of the world's population, 43% of world exports and 26% of world GDP.*

- *India adding 25 MM citizens to middle class each year equal to the population of Canada*

- *Japan's bilateral trade with China is now greater than its trade with America*

- *America's last MONTHLY trade surplus was during the Ford Administration and our Federal Government is spending $5 million a MINUTE*

- *According to KPMG—the least expensive places in the world to conduct business are Canada and Singapore*

- *Brazil's stock market is booming and it is energy sufficient due to use of sugarcane for ethanol production*

- *Taiwan and South Korea now export more to China than the US*

- *While GM debt relegated to junk bond status—80% of market value of global auto makers is accounted for by Nissan, Toyota and Honda. In July 2006, Toyota for the first time sold more cars in the US than Ford.*

China, India and other emerging markets are looking more like America at the turn of the 20th century. Many American business leaders seem to be preoccupied with short term goals rather than building lasting global empires.

Do we still have the best educated people in the world with plenty of incentives to discover, experiment, and create new and innovative products and services? With one third of our young people never finishing high school and a third of this unfortunate group never getting past ninth grade, we clearly have some work to do.

Many Americans feel in their bones that the energy, the momentum, the global dominance, the leadership, the economic independence, is waning instead of waxing. It seems that our prestige is slipping around the world.

A recent study by the Chicago Council on Global Affairs showed that 55% of Americans believed the US would be surpassed or equaled as a global power over the next 50 years. The Chinese polled see their country catching up with the U.S. in terms of global influence within ten years!

In short, many citizens and leaders in America are too comfortable and complacent. We face great challenges and opportunities to maintain our economic supremacy but we must act now and act boldly with imagination, creativity and courage.

America can create an economic environment that will allow it to retain and strengthen its global economic leadership and produce substantial economic growth that benefits all but it will have to face its challenges head on.

Today, I am going to put forth a blueprint of these reforms.

My goal is not to bury you in details which will need to be worked out through our political process. Rather, my objective is to capture your interest, motivate you to get involved and badger your elected representatives to think big and take the initiative to legislate economic reforms that will make a significant difference.

We have too many pie slicers in public life—more concerned with how to divide the pie and missing out on the big picture goal of making the pie larger. Then they add insult to injury by making pie crust promises—easily made and easily broken.

So let's forget petty politics and focus on some big ideas with an open and hopeful mind. These ideas should be judged not as left or right but rather as up or down, right or wrong.

And remember, unless an idea is big, it will pass like a ship in the night.

First, our current complicated tax system is like a clog in our national economic artery, slowing down investment, savings, incomes and growth. It could also be fatal to America's economic position in the world.

While politicians, lobbyists, tax accountants and lawyers may benefit from our tangled tax system, the rest of us lose—big time. This is especially true for our vast middle class who can ill afford to spend the money necessary to hire high priced legal and tax counsel expert at navigating the amazing complexity of our tax code.

In Washington, many legislators like a complex tax system so that they hand out favors, keep control and stay in power. Instead of concentrating on increasing the economic pie for all Americans, they take delight in wrangling over how the pie should be sliced.

As the distinguished former chairman of the U.S. Senate Finance Committee Russell Long put it, the attitude among many of us is "don't tax me, don't tax him, tax that man behind the tree."

It seems that every administration since the Johnson Administration—and I mean Andrew Johnson—has talked up a storm about tax simplification with very little to show for it. For example, President Carter's best campaign line—and the only one I might add—was to refer to our tax code as a "national disgrace" but nothing happened

His successor President Reagan did take a good whack at it with the Tax Reform Act of 1986 but since then—there have been 15,000 changes to the tax code.

U.S. households spend roughly 1% of GDP in complying with the income tax system. The U.S. Treasury Department estimates that, on average, the total tax burden on new corporate investment is 24%.

It is like when you prune the trees and bushes in your back yard. You cut them back one year but they grow right back. What we need to do is to uproot the tree and tax code—and start anew.

A simplified tax system will throw out the 9 million word tax code and replace it with a simple 15-17% tax rate that taxes income only once rather than two or three times.

Due to income exclusions of $12,000 per adult and $6,000 per child or dependent plus the retention of the mortgage interest deduction, the average family of four would not pay any taxes until their income exceeded $50,000 (roughly the 2006 median family income) and furthermore any interest on savings or dividend income would not be taxed at all.

Tax simplification will go a long way to unleash the creative genius of the American people and spur economic growth, productivity, savings, and investment.

Under the simple tax there is no tax on capital gains, no tax on social security benefits, no death taxes and no alternative minimum tax. Businesses would pay the same single corporate tax rate but be able to expense all business expenses including capital equipment in the year it was purchased to expand production in America.

Quite simply—a simple tax means more jobs, savings, investment and economic growth.

America is the world's largest and most entrepreneurial economy but it is increasingly losing ground to tough foreign competition. This has led to the erosion of its industrial base, weak growth in personal income, an $800 billion annual trade deficit, and a $500 billion budget deficit that is being financed by heavy borrowing from Japan's and China's central banks.

Furthermore, America's savings rate is negative and its tax rates are high relative to most industrialized countries and significantly higher than its dynamic foreign competitors.

The U.S. savings rate—the percentage of after-tax income that Americans save—has declined to worrisome levels. In 1984 it was 11% and in 2005 it dropped into negative territory meaning that Americans were spending more than they earned.

About 30% of American households have no financial assets and an additional 20% have insignificant holdings. In addition, households who have $2,000 or more in savings are ineligible for many welfare programs providing the poor with a disincentive to save. Furthermore, 40% of Americans don't have any tax liabilities and therefore do not respond to tax incentives.

It is important to highlight that the lack of a deep savings pool in America forces it to rely on overseas capital to finance its huge and growing budget deficits. This reduces our negotiating leverage and economic independence. A higher savings rate would also lead to lower levels of consumption and imports thus bringing our trade deficits under control.

This is not a new or untested idea—ten countries have already instituted a simple one rate tax system—America needs to get ahead of the curve with reform that simplifies the tax code, restrains Congressional spending and encourages savings and investment.

To recap, a simple tax will lead to lower interest rates, higher economic growth rate, a smaller budget deficit, more capital investments, more foreign direct investment, higher productivity, a higher savings rate and growth in real incomes due to more high quality jobs.

Next, let's turn to the spending side of the equation.

History shows that democracies often fail due to over extended finances and lack of fiscal discipline. Congress has and always will have a natural disposition to spending and a lack of political will to restrain it. Our budget deficit in 2006 will be more than $500 billion and the national debt has gone from $5.7 trillion in 2000 to over $8.5 trillion and is increasing at a rate of $1.6 billion a day.

President Reagan's comment that he doesn't worry much about the national debt because it's big enough to take care of itself was of course meant as a joke—but it just isn't very funny anymore. Perhaps more apt is <u>Chairman Mao's comment that it's always darkest before it is totally black.</u>

Congressional spending under the current administration is growing at a rate of 8%, double the inflation rate. Spending earmarks for specific pet projects by members of Congress have gone from 1,439 in 1995 to 13,998 in 2005.

This reminds me of a story I used to hear while I was working with the Joint Economic Committee and the U.S. Senate Finance Committee. A brand new Senator was advised by a long serving member how to have a long career in the U.S. Senate. His advice: <u>vote for every spending bill and against every tax hike.</u> Good thing I was in Washington just long enough to be inoculated and not long enough to be infected by this cynical beltway attitude,

In 2005, Congress passed a highway bill with 6,371 special projects costing the taxpayers $24 billion including the now famous $223 million bridge to nowhere.

<u>The Federal government is now spending $5 million per minute and borrowing $3 billion a day!</u> It seems clear that the system is broken.

More troubling is that we don't owe the debt to ourselves but 40% of our budget deficit is being financed by the central banks of China and Japan.

We have come a long way from Thomas Jefferson's attitude aptly captured in his statement: "I am for a government rigorously frugal and simple"

<u>The only viable solution is an indexed cap on federal spending based on inflation and population growth. In a time of crisis, it could only be overridden by a supermajority of 2/3 in both the Senate and the House.</u>

Now let's look at a few other important economic challenges.

We need to make sure we keep our global leadership in capital markets. <u>Our deep and broad financial markets are the envy of the world and the cornerstone of any market economy. Lately though, we seem to be slipping.</u> The United States has not been the world's best stock market in 16 years. In 2005, of the largest 25 initial public offerings, 24 were not registered in America. So far in 2006, of the largest 10 initial public offerings, 9 were not registered in America.

There are a number of reasons for this emerging problem. As one who worked with Enron in 1994-95 helping to finance energy projects, I, more than most, recognize the need to protect investors and make sure executives and board members fulfill their oversight responsibilities.

At the same time, we need to keep in mind the need for a regulatory balance and avoid overkill that may make our markets less attractive to the world. <u>If we drive the cost of compliance too high, U.S. and international companies will head to Europe and Asia to raise capital.</u>

For international companies, the cost of compliance with overlapping regulations, the potential cost of class action lawsuits plus the cost of reconciling to U.S. accounting standards may well tip the scales towards a London or Hong listing instead of New York.

<u>Related to this issue is the recent explosion in top executive pay which is oftentimes not related to management or stock performance.</u>

It is clearly undermining confidence in our capitalist system. It is largely due to a far too cozy relationship between the board of directors and the CEO. These CEOs do not put up any capital like entrepreneurs do and have little downside risk when taking these jobs—even if they are a complete failure.

Shareholder reforms are necessary to put the shareholder first and for shareholders to take an active role in selecting and approving board members.

Mutual and pension funds in particular have represent sizable shareholder power and need to exercise it on investors behalf. Here are a few proposals that would restore the shareholder, the owners of the company, to their rightful role in selecting and overseeing a company's board and, through the board, the CEO.

<u>We need to change the method of voting for board members</u>. Presently, companies put up a slate of directors and shareholders have two options: voting "yes" or "withhold". One "yes" vote was enough to get elected. This should be replaced by majority voting where a director needs more "yes" votes than "withhold" votes.

But board members need to be independent-minded and not just a proxy for an interest group such as a labor union or pension fund. European companies have tried this and it is a recipe for stalemate and chaos.

A bonus plan for a CEO should be based on returns that exceed the cost of capital rather than on increases in share price or earnings per share.

The awarding of restricted stock to CEOs should be quite limited since even a small increase in share price unrelated to a CEO's performance can yield big numbers. To earn restricted stock, CEOs should have to meet tough performance goals.

Vesting periods for restricted stock needs to be longer than the traditional three years. Five to ten years is more appropriate because a key goal of a CEO should be developing a management team that produces steady increases in shareholder wealth. Companies should also make their CEOs hold five to ten times their salaries in stock. In short, the future of a company's top executives should be tied closely to the fortunes of the company's shareholders.

<u>Americans also need to increase savings rates and to meet their retirement needs and to reduce the pressure on our social security system</u>. Younger Americans especially, should be given the option to place a portion of their contributions in a private investment account which they can manage.

Participation rates in employer-sponsored plans have declined over the last few years, especially among younger workers (ages 20 to 29) where the average participation rate is now below 40%. One practical solution is automatic enrollment, which channels a certain percentage of every worker's wages into a retirement plan, unless the worker opts out. The difference between an opt-in plan and an opt-out plan is huge. At Costco, for example, the participation rate in the first year automatic enrollment was offered rose to 78% from 61%.

Concentration of employer stock in defined contribution plans is risky. If the employer became insolvent, its workers would lose their jobs and much of their retirement income. A plan participant should be allowed to exchange employer stock into another investment option on a quarterly basis.

<u>At the same time, employers can help their workers save for retirement by adopting four practices that do not require legislative changes</u>. First, workers are more likely to save for retirement if they are afforded a reasonable array of investment options. Too much choice can be overwhelming.

In defined contribution plans offering 20 or fewer options, the average participation rate is 77%. By contrast, for those plans offering more than 20 investment options, the average participation rate falls to 66%.

Second, most workers do not realize that asset allocation is much more important than security selection in generating investment returns over the long term.

Employers can help solve this problem by offering "ready-mix" funds within their plans—including asset allocation funds that regularly rebalance, or lifestyle funds that gradually move their asset mix from stocks to bonds as participants near retirement.

Third, although the investment mix of a retirement portfolio should change over time, a plan should discourage participants from converting their portfolio mainly to bonds at retirement. There is a 50% chance that one member of a healthy couple, both age 65, will live to 92, and a 25% chance that one will live to 97. Given this long runway, an investment portfolio at retirement should contain a substantial percentage of stock funds.

Finally, if we want most Americans to have an adequate retirement income, we need to redefine the concept of retirement. Surveys of Baby Boomers show that roughly half expect to retire after age 65, and over two-thirds intend to work after they formally retire. Many will work for financial reasons, but a surprisingly large number will continue working to stay active in retirement. In response, employers should develop more flexible policies that allow their employees to work longer on a part-time basis.

Before turning to foreign economic policy there is just one more issue I would like to touch upon.

Consumer credit has been a wonderful option and helped fuel America's consumer economy but the credit card industry needs serious reform and much more transparency. The marketing of credit cards to college students, teaser rates, privacy issues and theft of identity, a dispute process tilted against the consumer, pages of fine print the consumer cannot understand and non-stop marketing and mailing of cards has all led to an explosion of credit card debt and millions of American families mired in debt.

There are few lobbies in Washington as powerful as the credit card and banking industry. The industry's most profitable customers, the ones being sought by creative marketing tactics, are the "revolvers:" the estimated 115 million Americans who carry monthly credit card debt.

The president of the American Bankers Association has publicly stated that revolvers are "the sweet spot" of the banking industry. This "sweet spot" continues to grow as the average credit card debt among American households has more than doubled over the past decade. Today, the average family owes roughly $8,000 on their credit cards. This *debt has helped generate record profits for the credit card industry—last year, more than $30 billion before taxes.*

Some experts say the profitability of credit cards really began 25 years ago when the banking industry successfully eliminated a critical restriction: the limit on the interest rate a lender can charge a borrower. Deregulation, coupled with a revolution in technology that enables the almost real-time tracking of personal financial information and the emergence of nationwide banking, has facilitated the widening availability of credit cards across the economic spectrum. But for most, the cost of credit is often far greater than it appears. a growing share of the industry's revenues come from what can be seen as deceptive tactics, such as "default" terms spelled out in the fine print of cardholder agreements—the terms and conditions of which can be changed at any time for any reason with 15 days' notice.

Penalty fees and rates are sometimes triggered by just a single lapse — a payment that arrives a couple of days or even hours late, a charge that exceeds the credit line by a few dollars, or a loan from another creditor which renders the cardholder "overextended" as defined by the nation's three powerful credit bureaus. This flurry of unexpected fees and rate hikes come just when consumers can least afford them.

The first logical step at reform is to make sure credit companies offer full disclosure and transparency. Marketing to college students and young people might also be restricted. Consumer credit has been a positive force in building a strong American economy but like everything else in life, too much of a good thing is harmful.

Now, let's turn to foreign policy with an emphasis on economic and trade policy.

First, freedom in all of its manifestations must be America's calling card. Free markets, freedom of religion, free press and a free press. But there is a limit to what degree we can impose freedom on other countries and above all we need to be consistent in calling for and encouraging countries to move in the direction of more freedom for their people.

America should stand ready to help people fighting for their freedom but make it abundantly clear that we will not do their fighting for them.

While the world is much freer than it was twenty years ago, there is much more to be done. Take for example the United Nations. The United Nations is a flawed institution primarily because of its nebulous mission and lack of membership criteria. Chartwell America's United Nations of Freedom Project is an organization with the clear mission of promoting freedom by recognizing countries that are making a commitment to economic, political and religious freedom.

Of the 192 current member countries, more than 70 do not have a democratic form of government and the group of G-77 votes as a bloc and easily mobilizing majorities to block reforms in the General Assembly and other U.N. bodies. Finally, you have the problem of two permanent members of the U.N. Security Council that have little respect for individual freedoms and democracy.

Secondly, despite clear evidence of Asia's growing importance, <u>America's foreign policy establishment is still too Euro-centric.</u>

It is high time that we fully engage Asia. Asia represents 48% of the world's population, heavyweights like Japan, China and India plus 850 million people and $1 trillion in GDP from ASEAN countries including the largest Muslim country in the world—Indonesia. One example of the lack of attention was President Bush's recent trip to Southeast Asia. He spent only one day in Indonesia, not even spending one night in the country.

America needs to rebalance its focus, attention and resources to Asia. Specifically, the priorities need to be the following:

<u>Deepen our relationship with</u> Japan in economic, cultural and security matters as the cornerstone of our Asian strategy.

<u>Promote closer relations with India</u> including support of democracy, increased levels of trade, security cooperation, and market reforms to increase foreign investment and economic growth.

<u>Revitalize our involvement with ASEAN countries</u> and seek to participate in the emerging ASEAN Trade Bloc. Of particular interest is doing what we can to strengthen democracy in Indonesia and increase economic cooperation.

Next to the conflict with radical Islam, there is no more important foreign policy issue than understanding and dealing with the challenge presented by China.

<u>When historians look back on the 21st century, my bet is that the rise of India and China and America's response will eclipse the challenge of radical Islam as the defining theme of the century.</u>

Because of the war on terrorism, China is getting a free pass despite moving in the wrong direction on many issues such as freedom of religion, freedom of the press, privatization of its state-owned companies, open markets and democracy.

I don't agree on much with new House Speaker Nancy Pelosi but do agree with her hawkish comment that "wishing for the best is not a sound China policy".

China's goal is quite straightforward and clear, to become the hegemonic power in Asia and a leading global power—which it believes to be its rightful historic role. To achieve this goal it needs to build a strong economy and military and gradually weaken the role played in Asia by America and Japan.

That China has these ambitions would not be cause for concern if it was an open, pluralistic, democratic and private enterprise country. But it is not and despite the belief of many policymakers hoping for reform in these areas China is unlikely to move towards meaningful reform in any of these areas.

The reason is that the Chinese Communist Party's overriding goal is to maintain power while it strengthens China's economy and seeks hegemony in Asia.

While Chinese companies want to operate freely in a private enterprise global economy, most of the Chinese economy and certainly the leading companies will remain in state hands. Religious freedom, a free press and an open media and society are seen as a threat to its power and control.

America needs to accept these truths and form a realistic China policy that protects its interests and stands on the side of freedom, reform and private enterprise. Right now the commercial challenge from China is on the front burner. We need to use the principal of reciprocity to open more markets in China for American firms. The window to use our superior leverage due to the size of our consumer markets is closing fast and the Chinese realize this. The longer they can stall and negotiate, the better their negotiating stance.

China is already the third largest economy in the world with the third largest military budget. It is using its growing clout to expand its relationships with and selling arms to America's adversaries in Africa and the Middle East, and specifically Sudan and Iran. It seems clear that a Sino-Russian alliance is blossoming and China is exploiting our preoccupation with the Middle East to strengthen commercial alliances in America's backyard, Latin America.

The rise of Asia and in particular China presents America with the largest economic challenge in its history. On the economic front, China's substantial low cost advantage, economies of scale and entrepreneurial energy translate into extreme competitive pressure on American companies, workers and the U.S. industrial base. Our trade deficit with China alone exceeded $200 billion in 2005 and the China Central Bank is financing almost 30% of our budget deficit by purchasing U.S. Treasury bonds. In addition, the great majority of leading Chinese companies are state-owned.

America's industrial base is getting weaker and we need to make the U.S. a leading manufacturer and exporter of sophisticated high value added products once more. This is the only way to generate high paying jobs and foster support for open trade. Without a vibrant and growing economy, the resources required to protect America's vital interests around the world will not be forthcoming. A strong defense depends on a healthy economy.

As the breadbasket of the world, The U.S. is well positioned to expand its agricultural exports which now account for about 30% of our total agricultural output.

America's most important asset in negotiating trade and economic agreements is our huge consumer market. While participating in global trade organizations, we should not hesitate to negotiate advantageous bi-lateral agreements using continued access to US consumer markets as negotiating leverage. A major goal should be to open global agricultural, consumer, and financial markets to American products and services.

American exports support one out in five U.S. manufacturing jobs and jobs tied directly to exports pay 15% higher wages than other jobs. Agricultural exports now account for 925,000 American jobs.

The Chinese are using just the hope of accessing their consumer market to force American and European multinational to manufacture in China, share intellectual capital and invest in Chinese projects. We already have the market but do not use the enormous negotiating leverage we have in our hands.

It is also shortsighted to think that America can keep its position in the world marketplace by drifting to a service only economy. Manufacturing is the foundation of all wealth creation.

But even though America now has more workers with state and local governments than directly engaged in manufacturing, all is not bleak. According to a recent article in the Wall Street Journal, the United States remains the world's largest manufacturer—$1.8

trillion worth of output in 2005—more than twice that of Japan. Still it is only 15% of American GDP compared to 42% for China.

Having said all this, I do not mean to imply that the American worker can compete at the low end with foreign workers making a $1 an hour. Rather we need to emulate the Japanese model. <u>Outsource the low end but ferociously defend the sophisticated high end product manufacturing and at the same time protect the intellectual capital and R&D work by keeping it at home. Concentrate on products that are time-sensitive, complex and intricate and difficult to move around.</u>

America need a portfolio approach to manufacturing with the low end offshore and products and research that demands constant innovation at home. A more robust trade policy, the simple tax, cutting back excessive regulation and litigation are all part of the puzzle that will maintain and strengthen our vital manufacturing base.

<u>Another top priority must be to protect our hard earned intellectual property rights and capital.</u> If countries continue to tolerate the rampant theft of intellectual property and counterfeiting we should consider penalties as a form of compensation.

<u>It seems to me that a fair principle of economic relations with other countries is reciprocity.</u> If U.S. consumer markets are open to a country's exports, U.S. exports must have free access to their markets. If overseas private companies can invest freely in American companies and capital markets, American firms should have similar privileges. A policy of mercantilism by some of our trading partners is weakening our economic base and undermining U.S. support for open markets.

And let me say that a weaker U.S. dollar is not a solution to current trade imbalances. <u>No great country has ever maintained its greatness by debasing its currency.</u> In fact, a weaker dollar leads directly to a cut in American wealth and wages. The U.S. dollar's fate is in our hands and the right economic and foreign policies will keep it strong.

<u>Meanwhile much closer to home is our most underutilized foreign policy asset: American generosity</u>. Americans are the most generous people in the world in donating their money, time and talent to philanthropic organizations. In 2005, Americans donated $260 billion with 76% coming from individuals who on average donated 2.2% of their income.

By most measures, Americans remain the most charitable people world-wide. In 2005, giving in the U.S. averaged 1.75% of gross domestic product, according to the

Charities Aid Foundation, compared to 0.75% in Britain, and in Germany, France and Singapore, the rate of giving was about 0.25% of GDP last year.

Rather than softening the face of American power, this generosity is neither understood nor appreciated by the world.

Why is this? Part of the problem is that we don't do a very good job packaging and drawing attention to our goodwill efforts.

One example of this problem goes way back to the Eisenhower Administration. Secretary of State John Foster Dulles visited India bearing a gift of $50 million (this was big bucks at the time) and this sizable gift garnered only the slightest attention and was promptly buried in the back of the newspapers. But the great showman Soviet leader Nikita Khrushchev upstaged Dulles by sending Nehru a magnificent white horse as a gift. Needless to say, the gift horse dominated the front page of all the newspapers for weeks on end.

We need to be much more creative in making our generosity come alive. Instead of a $10 million gift why not school lunches for 1 million malnourished children, 100,000 mosquito nets that save thousands from malaria or 10 million gallons of fresh water that saves 10,000 infants from death through dehydration?

It seems obvious that the great majority of private charitable organizations are well run, cost effective and entrepreneurial. They are also experts in their specialties and close to the people they are trying to help.

All contributions to these organizations should be tax free and government organizations whose missions overlap with private charities should allow them to lead and manage programs limiting their role to matching private contributions.

One example is the U.S. Agency for International Development (USAID) which has an annual budget of about $10 billion. Rather than fund and try to manage development projects all over the world, let's use this USAID money to match funds raised by private American foundations and charitable organizations.

According to Giving USA, about $100 billion of American charitable contributions were for global causes such as economic development, medical research and disaster assistance. Global aid projects will be run much more efficiently and the goodwill generated by these organizations as they help people around the globe will transform America's image abroad.

As the breadbasket of the world, America is also in a position to distribute agricultural products to more than 800 million of the world's six billion plus people are unable to obtain the adequate, nutritious food needed for sound health and growth.

Such undernourishment negatively affects people's health and productivity. According to the World Health Organization, poor nutrition causes one in three people to die prematurely or have disabilities. Among young children the impact is even greater—malnutrition is a contributing factor in more than 50 percent of deaths among children under the age of five worldwide.

The potential exists to use American agricultural surpluses to greatly expand the American Red Cross's nutrition initiatives. For example, in Vietnam, four million elementary school children are malnourished. Providing food in school to students every day as well as take-tome food rations to families of students act as incentives for children to attend school.

The take-home ration, while also nutritious, helps offset families' financial expenditures on food. America can lead a revolution in entrepreneurial philanthropy at home and around the globe. It is already the global leader but receives precious little goodwill.

Consider this question—if Brazil can become energy self sufficient and independent—why can't America. In fact, let's think big and go one step further with the goal of becoming a net energy exporter.

By promoting renewable energy, conservation, clean coal technologies and expanding nuclear and hydrogen based power we can achieve this goal within a decade. It has to be easier than putting a man on the moon.

America's dependence on oil is a critical strategic weakness that must be addressed—and fast.

The US transportation system is 97% dependent on oil and more than 90% of the world oil supply is controlled by foreign governments—many of them unstable and hostile to U.S. interests.

America needs to take an active leadership role in developing massive amounts of nuclear energy for its own use as well as for export. Paul Johnson points out that America's aircraft carriers and submarines are almost entirely powered by nuclear reactors with sterling safety records.

We have the technical expertise and the financing capability to build large scale, safe and secure nuclear generators that could be located in protected remote areas.

In December, 1951, America developed the first nuclear reactor in Idaho which generated enough electricity to light four 200 watt bulbs. There are now 438 commercial nuclear reactors in the world which provide 16% of global electricity. In the United States, we have 104 reactors which provide 20% of our electricity needs.

But since 1979, no American utility has applied for a new nuclear power plant construction permit. Meanwhile, 80% of France's power comes from nuclear power plants and India and China has nuclear power at the center of their energy plans. India plans on adding eight nuclear plants from 2005-2010 and China, which now relies on coal for 70% of their energy needs, plans to build 40 nuclear reactors from 2005-2020.

Britain has decided to build a large number of new power plants and Finland is following suit. There are issues of disposal of waste but no doubt this challenge can be overcome.

America would benefit greatly from taking a global leadership role in generating clean energy. Lowering costs, cleaner air, export revenues and of course, less dependency on Middle Eastern oil. Keep in mind that 50% of the world's natural gas reserves are in Russia and Iran. America can and must be energy independent.

Lastly, even if we push forward all the reforms we have discussed today, we ill fall short if we don't improve American education.

A recent report by a blue ribbon panel selected by the National Center on Education and the Economy can be summed up by a key statistic:

Only 18 out of 100 American high school freshmen will graduate from high school on time, enroll directly in college and earn a two-year degree in three years or a four-year degree in six years.

There is no way America can stay competitive with this sort of performance.

In almost every classroom across America, teachers face the same dilemma. Of the say 25 students in a class, five are ready to race ahead and five need special attention and tutoring. Currently, teachers have little choice but to teach to the middle leading to two serious problems. The best students are held back and the struggling students become frustrated and fall way behind. America can ill afford to waste the talents of gifted students nor the tragedy of students that eventually drop out due to discouragement.

The results are not a pretty picture. According to the National Assessment of Educational Progress, only 30% of eight graders are "proficient" or "advanced" in reading. 30% of American students do not finish high school. American children on average spend 900 hours each year in the classroom and 1,023 hours in front of the television. In China, nearly all high school students study advanced calculus and biology. In Bangalore India, it is commonplace for eight grade students to study algebra. By the time our students reach ninth grade, they are already two years behind Singapore students.

Resources are always an issue but high expectations plus parent and teacher attention, attitude and effort are just as if not more important. America spends far more than any other country on education with very poor returns.

While many things have changed and evolved in America, our schools seem to amble along blissfully unaware that they are outdated, inefficient and unresponsive to the needs of children. If Rip Van Winkle awoke after a 50 year nap and visited a school— little would surprise him.

One idea is to change the way we look at computers and balance traditional teaching methods with increasingly innovative learning software available in the marketplace.

Why not turn "computer labs" into "learning centers" where advanced student can go for supplemental challenging coursework and students who need extra help can go for tutoring and special help?

The tragedy is that in many schools, the infrastructure is right there but it is not being used. Teachers need to be trained and the logistics of moving students through the learning centers needs to be better developed.

This is also a way to broaden the curriculum at with very little incremental cost. Want to learn Chinese, Japanese, German or Spanish—Rosetta Stone interactive software is at your fingertips. Innovative and fun math, reading, science programs are also easily accessible. Starting these programs in kindergarten will help fix problems early and avoid the huge costs of remedial classes later on not to mention the infinite cost of drop outs.

Another great idea is "weighted student funding" where each child receives a "back-pack" of education funding that travels with him to the school of his or hers family _choice_. *Principals and teachers, with parental involvement, would then have the freedom to spend this backpack as they see fit to help the child.*

Finally, while each student needs to master the gateway skills of reading, writing and arithmetic, we need to realize that <u>America's hallmark has been to use these skills creatively to innovate and that this has been the secret of our economic success.</u>

In today's ever more demanding and competitive global economy, new products and services will come from teams combining technology, art and design. We need to look forward, not back, to focus not just on basic math, English and science but to emphasize, flexibility, imagination, creativity and innovation in all subjects including foreign languages, the arts and the other humanities.

In the end, all the tests, resources and new teaching methods will be for naught if our students don't have a positive attitude towards learning and are not ambitious to achieve. Parents, teachers and students need to radiate enthusiasm for learning.

<u>*So there we have it: a simple tax, federal spending caps, shifting foreign economic policy focus to Asia, a forward leaning trade policy which opens markets, maintaining global financial leadership, energy independence, education reform and corporate reform to maintain faith in our free enterprise system.*</u>

Perhaps some will say that these reforms are too ambitious and unrealistic but think of the challenges that faced our newborn nation and they pale in comparison. Our first and best Treasury Secretary Alexander Hamilton oozed with ambition, energy and imagination.

As the architect of America's corporate free enterprise system, Hamilton laid its foundation by building a national currency, establishing property rights, a system of public credit, a tax and customs system not to mention a comprehensive proposal for our first central bank.

<u>*All of this in fifteen months!*</u> *Mr. Hamilton looked ahead and saw the America we enjoy today.*

What do our leaders see as America's future?

Americans, I am convinced, are ready for action. The question is whether our leaders are ready? The path of great leadership does not lie along the top of a fence. We need to confront our problems, think through what we need to do to keep America on top, and then jump over the fence with faith and courage.

And what if we do our best and come up short of our goals?

William Penn put it well: "To have striven, to have made the effort, to have been true to certain ideals—this alone is worth the struggle."

In closing, there are some who say it doesn't matter if the world's financial capital is Shanghai rather than New York. Nor whether the global leader in technology is India and the cutting edge of manufacturing rests in Japan.

We must emphatically reject this complacency and defeatism.

That we do so is not important only to America but to the world. Abraham Lincoln put it well in his eulogy for Henry Clay in 1852:

"(Mr. Clay) loved his country ... mostly because it was a free country; and he burned with a zeal for its advancement, prosperity and glory, because he saw in such, the advancement, prosperity and glory, of human liberty, human rights and human nature. He desired the prosperity of his countrymen partly because they were his countrymen, but chiefly to show to the world that freemen could be prosperous."

Sure, we have some work to do but I for one believe that the best is yet to come.

America's ace in the hole is our openness, optimism and flexibility.

Let's confound the skeptics and the cynics.

If we put the reforms outlined in this speech put into place, America's leadership, prosperity and values will stay strong and spread throughout the world.

The ETF Library

ETFs on the Market

iShares GS$ InvesTop Corp Bond	LQD	Bond—Corporate
iShares Lehman 1-3Yr Treasury Bond	SHY	Bond—Government
iShares Lehman 20+Yr Treasury Bond	TLT	Bond—Government
iShares Lehman 7-10Yr Treasury Bond	IEF	Bond—Government
iShares Lehman TIPS Bond Fund	TIP	Bond—Government
iShares Lehman Aggregate Fund	AGG	Bond—Multisector
BLDRS Emerging Market 50 ADR Index	ADRE	Emerging Market Equity
iShares MSCI Emerging Markets Index	EEM	Emerging Market Equity
Vanguard Emerging Markets VIPERs	VWO	Emerging Market Equity
iShares S&P Global 100	IOO	Global Equity
iShares S&P Global Technology Sect	IXN	Global Equity
iShares S&P Global Telecomm Sect	IXP	Global Equity
streetTRACKS DJ Global Titan	DGT	Global Equity
HOLDRS Market 2000 +	MKH	Global Equity
iShares NYSE Composite Index Fund	NYC	Market Index
iShares S&P 1500 Index Fund	ISI	Market Index
Diamond Series Trust I	DIA	Market Index
Fidelity Nasdaq Comp Tracker Stock	ONEQ	Market Index
PowerShares Dynamic OTC Portfolio	PWO	Market Index
PowerShares Dynamic Market Portf	PWC	Market Index
Vanguard Extended Market VIPERs	VXF	Market Index
iShares Russell 3000 Growth	IWZ	Mkt. Index—Growth
iShares S&P 500/Barra Growth	IVW	Mkt. Index—Growth
iShares NYSE 100 Index Fund	NY	Mkt. Index—Large
iShares S&P 100 Index Fund	OEF	Mkt. Index—Large
iShares Russell 1000	IWB	Mkt. Index—Large
iShares S&P 500	IVV	Mkt. Index—Large
SPDR 500	SPY	Mkt. Index—Large
Vanguard Large Cap VIPERs	VV	Mkt. Index—Large
iShares Morningstar Large Core	JKD	Mkt. Index—Large Core
Rydex Russell Top 50 ETF	XLG	Mkt. Index—Large Core
streetTRACKS SPDR O-STRIP ETF	OOO	Mkt. Index—Large Growth
iShares Morningstar Large Growth	JKE	Mkt. Index—Large Growth
iShares Russell 1000 Growth	IWF	Mkt. Index—Large Growth

PowerShares Dynamic Lg Cap Growth	PWB	Mkt. Index—Large Growth
streetTRACKS DJ US Lg Cap Growth	ELG	Mkt. Index—Large Growth
Vanguard Growth VIPERs	VUG	Mkt. Index—Large Growth
iShares Morningstar Large Value	JKF	Mkt. Index—Large Value
iShares Russell 1000 Value	IWD	Mkt. Index—Large Value
PowerShares Dynamic Large Cap Value	PWV	Mkt. Index—Large Value
Rydex S&P Equal Weight ETF	RSP	Mkt. Index—Large Value
Vanguard Value VIPERs	VTV	Mkt. Index—Large Value
streetTRACKS DJ US Lg Cap Value	ELV	Mkt. Index—Large Value
iShares Russell Microcap Index Fund	IWC	Mkt. Index—Microcap
PowerShares Zacks Micro Cap	PZI	Mkt. Index—Microcap
iShares Russell Midcap Index	IWR	Mkt. Index—Mid
iShares S&P MidCap 400	IJH	Mkt. Index—Mid
Vanguard Mid Cap VIPERs	VO	Mkt. Index—Mid
SPDR Mid Cap 400	MDY	Mkt. Index—Mid
iShares Morningstar Mid Growth	JKH	Mkt. Index—Mid Growth
iShares Russell Midcap Growth Index	IWP	Mkt. Index—Mid Growth
iShares S&P MidCap 400/Barra Growth	IJK	Mkt. Index—Mid Growth
PowerShares Dynamic Mid Cap Growth	PWJ	Mkt. Index—Mid Growth
iShares Morningstar Mid Core	JKG	Mkt. Index—Mid Value
iShares Morningstar Mid Value	JKI	Mkt. Index—Mid Value
iShares Russell Midcap Value Index	IWS	Mkt. Index—Mid Value
iShares S&P MidCap 400/Barra Value	IJJ	Mkt. Index—Mid Value
PowerShares Dynamic Mid Cap Value	PWP	Mkt. Index—Mid Value
iShares Russell 2000	IWM	Mkt. Index—Small
iShares S&P SmallCap 600	IJR	Mkt. Index—Small
Vanguard Small Cap VIPERs	VB	Mkt. Index—Small
iShares Morningstar Small Core	JKJ	Mkt. Index—Small
iShares Morningstar Small Growth	JKK	Mkt. Index—Small Growth
iShares Russell 2000 Growth	IWO	Mkt. Index—Small Growth
iShares S&P SmallCap 600/Barra Gwth	IJT	Mkt. Index—Small Growth
PowerShares Dynamic Sm Cap Growth	PWT	Mkt. Index—Small Growth
streetTRACKS DJ US Small Cap Growth	DSG	Mkt. Index—Small Growth
Vanguard Small Cap Growth VIPERs	VBK	Mkt. Index—Small Growth

iShares Morningstar Small Value	JKL	Mkt. Index—Small Value
iShares Russell 2000 Value	IWN	Mkt. Index—Small Value
iShares S&P SmallCap 600/BarraValue	IJS	Mkt. Index—Small Value
PowerShares Dynamic Small Cap Value	PWY	Mkt. Index—Small Value
streetTRACKS DJ US Small Cap Value	DSV	Mkt. Index—Small Value
Vanguard Small Cap Value VIPERs	VBR	Mkt. Index—Small Value
iShares Dow Jones US Total Mkt	IYY	Mkt. Index—Total Mkt.
iShares Russell 3000	IWV	Mkt. Index—Total Mkt.
Vanguard Total Stock Market VIPERs	VTI	Mkt. Index—Total Mkt.
streetTRACKS Total Market ETF	TMW	Mkt. Index—Total Mkt.
iShares Russell 3000 Value	IWW	Mkt. Index—Value
iShares S&P 500/Barra Value	IVE	Mkt. Index—Large Value
BLDRS Asia 50 ADR Index	ADRA	Non-US Equity
BLDRS Developed Mkts 100 ADR Index	ADRD	Non-US Equity
BLDRS Europe 100 ADR Index	ADRU	Non-US Equity
HOLDRS Europe 2001	EKH	Non-US Equity
HOLDRS TeleBras	TBH	Non-US Equity
iShares FTSE/Xinhua China 25	FXI	Non-US Equity
iShares MSCI Australia Index	EWA	Non-US Equity
iShares MSCI Austria Index	EWO	Non-US Equity
iShares MSCI Belgium Index	EWK	Non-US Equity
iShares MSCI Brazil Index	EWZ	Non-US Equity
iShares MSCI Canada Index	EWC	Non-US Equity
iShares MSCI EAFE Growth Index Fund	EFG	Non-US Equity
iShares MSCI EAFE Index Fund	EFA	Non-US Equity
iShares MSCI EAFE Value Index Fund	EFV	Non-US Equity
iShares MSCI EMU Index	EZU	Non-US Equity
iShares MSCI France Index	EWQ	Non-US Equity
iShares MSCI Germany Index	EWG	Non-US Equity
iShares MSCI Hong Kong Index	EWH	Non-US Equity
iShares MSCI Italy Index	EWI	Non-US Equity
iShares MSCI Japan Index	EWJ	Non-US Equity
iShares MSCI Malaysia Index	EWM	Non-US Equity
iShares MSCI Mexico Index	EWW	Non-US Equity

iShares MSCI Netherlands Index	EWN	Non-US Equity
iShares MSCI Pacific ex-Japan Idx	EPP	Non-US Equity
iShares MSCI Singapore Index	EWS	Non-US Equity
iShares MSCI South Africa	EZA	Non-US Equity
iShares MSCI South Korea Index	EWY	Non-US Equity
iShares MSCI Spain Index	EWP	Non-US Equity
iShares MSCI Sweden Index	EWD	Non-US Equity
iShares MSCI Switzerland Index	EWL	Non-US Equity
iShares MSCI Taiwan Index	EWT	Non-US Equity
iShares MSCI UK Index	EWU	Non-US Equity
iShares S&P Europe 350 Index Fund	IEV	Non-US Equity
iShares S&P Latin American 40 Idx	ILF	Non-US Equity
iShares S&P/Topix 150 Index Fund	ITF	Non-US Equity
PowerShares Gldn Drgn Hltr USX Chn	PGJ	Non-US Equity
streetTRACKS EURO STOXX 50	FEZ	Non-US Equity
streetTRACKS STOXX 50	FEU	Non-US Equity
Vanguard European VIPERs	VGK	Non-US Equity
Vanguard Pacific VIPERs	VPL	Non-US Equity
HOLDRS Broadband	BDH	Sector—Broadband
Vanguard Consumer Discret VIPERs	VCR	Sector—Consumer
Vanguard Consumer Staples VIPERs	VDC	Sector—Consumer
iShares Dow Jones US Cns Gd Sct Idx	IYK	Sector—Consumer
iShares Dow Jones US Cns Sv Sct Idx	IYC	Sector—Consumer
SPDR Consumer Discretionary	XLY	Sector—Consumer
SPDR Consumer Staples	XLP	Sector—Consumer
HOLDRS Oil Services	OIH	Sector—Energy/Natural Res
iShares Dow Jones US Energy Sector	IYE	Sector—Energy/Natural Res
iShares Goldman Sachs Nat Res Index	IGE	Sector—Energy/Natural Res
iShares S&P Global Energy Sector	IXC	Sector—Energy/Natural Res
PowerShares Wilder Clean Energy	PBW	Sector—Energy/Natural Res
SPDR Energy	XLE	Sector—Energy/Natural Res
Vanguard Energy VIPERs	VDE	Sector—Energy/Natural Res
HOLDRS Regional Bank	RKH	Sector—Financial Services
iShares Dow Jones US Financial Sct	IYF	Sector—Financial Services

iShares Dow Jones US Financial Srv	IYG	Sector—Financial Services
iShares S&P Global Financials Sect	IXG	Sector—Financial Services
SPDR Financial	XLF	Sector—Financial Services
Vanguard Financials VIPERs	VFH	Sector—Financial Services
PowerShares Dynamic Food & Beverage	PBJ	Sector—Food & Bev.
SPDR Health Care	XLV	Sector—Health/Biotechnology
HOLDRS Biotech	BBH	Sector—Health/Biotechnology
HOLDRS Pharmaceutical	PPH	Sector—Health/Biotechnology
iShares Biotechnology Index Fund	IBB	Sector—Health/Biotechnology
iShares Dow Jones US Healthcare	IYH	Sector—Health/Biotechnology
iShares S&P Global Healthcare Sect	IXJ	Sector—Health/Biotechnology
PowerShares Dynamic Biotech&Genome	PBE	Sector—Health/Biotechnology
PowerShares Dynamic Pharmaceuticals	PJP	Sector—Health/Biotechnology
Vanguard Health Care VIPERs	VHT	Sector—Health/Biotechnology
Vanguard Industrials VIPERs	VIS	Sector—Industrials
iShares Dow Jones US Industrial	IYJ	Sector—Industrials
SPDR Industrial	XLI	Sector—Industrials
HOLDRS B2B Internet	BHH	Sector—Internet
HOLDRS Internet	HHH	Sector—Internet
HOLDRS Internet Infrastructure	IIH	Sector—Internet
HOLDRS Internet Architecture	IAH	Sector—Internet
PowerShares Dynamic Leisure&Entert	PEJ	Sector—Leisure & Ent.
Vanguard Materials VIPERs	VAW	Sector—Materials
iShares Dow Jones US Basic Mtrls	IYM	Sector—Materials
SPDR Materials	XLB	Sector—Materials
PowerShares Dynamic Media	PBS	Sector—Media
PowerShares Dynamic Networking	PXQ	Sector—Networking
iShares Goldman Sachs Ntwr Index Fd	IGN	Sector—Networking
iShares Comex Gold Trust	IAU	Sector—Precious Metals
streetTRACKS Gold Shares	GLD	Sector—Precious Metals
iShares Cohen&Steers Realty Major	ICF	Sector—Real Estate
iShares Dow Jones US Real Estate	IYR	Sector—Real Estate
streetTRACKS Wilshire REIT	RWR	Sector—Real Estate
Vanguard REIT VIPERs	VNQ	Sector—Real Estate

HOLDRS Retail	RTH	Sector—Retail
PowerShares Dynamic Semiconductor	PSI	Sector—Semicon
HOLDRS Semiconductor	SMH	Sector—Semicon
iShares Goldman Sachs Semicon Index	IGW	Sector—Semicon
HOLDRS Software	SWH	Sector—Software
iShares Goldman Sachs Software Indx	IGV	Sector—Software
PowerShares Dynamic Software Portf	PSJ	Sector—Software
iShares Dow Jones US Technology	IYW	Sector—Technology
iShares Goldman Sachs Technology	IGM	Sector—Technology
Nasdaq 100 Trust Series I	QQQQ	Sector—Technology
SPDR Technology	XLK	Sector—Technology
streetTRACKS MS Technology Index	MTK	Sector—Technology
Vanguard Information Tech VIPERs	VGT	Sector—Technology
HOLDRS Telecom	TTH	Sector—Telecom
iShares Dow Jones US Telecom	IYZ	Sector—Telecom
Vanguard Telecom Serv VIPERs	VOX	Sector—Telecom
iShares Dow Jones Transportation	IYT	Sector—Transport
HOLDRS Utilities	UTH	Sector—Utilities
iShares Dow Jones US Utilities	IDU	Sector—Utilities
SPDR Utilities	XLU	Sector—Utilities
Vanguard Utilities VIPERs	VPU	Sector—Utilities
HOLDRS Wireless	WMH	Sector—Wireless
iShares DJ US Select Dividend Index	DVY	Specialty—Dividend
PowerShares High Yld Eq Div Ach	PEY	Specialty—Dividend
iShares KLD Select Social SM Index	KLD	Specialty—Social

ETF Sponsors

iShares
Barclays Global Investors
http://www.ishares.com

Powershares
Powershares Capital Management
http://www.powershares.com

Vanguard ETFs
Vanguard Investments
http://wwww.vanguard.com

Spiders
ALPS Distributors
http://www.spdrindex.com
http://amex.com/spy

StreetTracks
State Street Global Investors
http://advisors.ssga.com/etf/index

Wisdom Tree
Wisdomtree Investments
http://www.wisdomtree.com

HOLDRS
Merrill Lynch
http://www.holdrs.com

Rydex ETFs
Rydex Investments
http://rydexfunds.com/etfs/

Rydex Currency Shares
http://currencyshares.com

ProShares
Proshares Advisors LLC
http://www.proshares.com

First Trust
First Trust Portfolios, LP
http://www.firsttrustportfolios.com/

Claymore
Claymore Securities
http://claymore.com

ETF Investment Glossary

After-tax Returns
After-tax returns are based on the historical highest individual federal marginal income tax rates and do not reflect state and local taxes. Actual after-tax returns depend on the investor's tax situation and may be higher or lower. The after-tax returns shown are not relevant to investors who hold their fund shares through tax-deferred arrangements such as IRAs or 401(k) plans.

Alpha
manager's return relative to the return of a benchmark.

Asset Allocation
The process of spreading an investment among various asset classes such as stocks, bonds, and cash equivalents with the goal of reducing portfolio volatility and increasing long term returns.

Barclays Global Investors (BGI)
Barclays Global Investors is the creator of iShares® and is a wholly owned subsidiary of Barclays Bank PLC. BGI is one of the world's largest investment managers and created the world's first index strategy more than thirty years ago.

Basis Point
A unit of measure, equal to 1/100th of 1%, or .01%. 100 basis points = 1%

Capitalization-Weighted Index

This an index that gives each company a weight in proportion to the total market value of that company's outstanding shares. The vast majority of indices today are constructed in this manner.

Cohen & Steers

Founded in 1986, Cohen & Steers was the first American company formed exclusively to focus on real estate securities. The firm was founded with the belief that a well-managed portfolio of publicly traded real estate investment trusts (REITs) and other real estate companies can offer investors the beneficial investment characteristics of direct real estate ownership.

Cohen & Steers Realty Majors Index

The Cohen & Steers Realty Majors Index consists of selected Real Estate Investment Trusts (REITs). The objective of the index is to represent relatively large and liquid REITs that may benefit from future consolidation and securitization of the U.S. real estate industry. The index is weighted according to the total market value of each REIT's outstanding shares and is adjusted quarterly so that no REIT represents more than 8% of the index.

Core/Satellite Hypothetical Tool

The Core/Satellite tool allows you to hypothetically illustrate the tradeoff between alpha and tracking error to a benchmark index. Intuitively, active managers can potentially achieve higher alpha with higher levels of tracking error since higher tracking errors reflect the fact that the manager's portfolio is increasingly different than the benchmark. However, client tolerance for tracking error varies based on their individual tolerance for under performing a benchmark over the near- or long-term. The Core/Satellite tool serves as a calculator for illustrating a hypothetical portfolio that blends indexes with active managers to achieve a lower tracking error than that produced by an allocation entirely to the active manager. There are three key inputs for the Core/Satellite tool: Alpha, Tracking Error and Active Manager Risk Budget.

Exchange-Traded Funds

Exchange-traded funds (**ETFs**) are not mutual funds in the traditional sense; rather, they are hybrid instruments combining aspects of common stocks and mutual funds and offering many of the benefits of both. Created in 1993, these instruments have been widely used by institutional investors (some 75% of the universe of **ETF** assets, now more than $400 billion, is held by institutions) and retail investors.

Free-Float
Free-float refers to the amount of a company's shares outstanding that are available for purchase on the open market at any point in time

Growth-Oriented Stocks
Stocks of companies that have shown faster-than-average gains in earnings over several years and are expected to continue to show high levels of profit growth. Typically riskier than average stocks, they exhibit higher price/earnings ratios and often make little or no dividend payments to shareholders.

Index
An index is a composite of a group of stocks and is used as a barometer of a market and as a benchmark for investors. Today, there are thousands of indices and some of the indices that iShares track are Russell, S&P, MSCI, Dow Jones and Lehman Brothers.

Index-Tracking Shares
Index-tracking shares are not mutual funds in the traditional sense; rather, they are hybrid instruments combining aspects of common stocks and mutual funds and offering many the benefits of both.

Internal Rate of Return (IRR)
Internal Rate of Return (IRR) is the discount rate at which the present value of the future cash flows of an investment equal the cost of the investment. It is found by a process of trial and error; when the net present values of cash outflows (the cost of the investment) and cash inflows (returns on the investment) equal zero, the rate of discount being used is the IRR.

Large-Cap U.S. Companies
Generally speaking, companies with market capitalization greater than $10 billion.

MSCI Indexes
The Morgan Stanley Capital International (MSCI) indexes are constructed in a consistent manner across all countries, encompassing a total of 23 developed markets and 28 emerging markets. This consistent approach to index construction ensures the proper representation of the countries' underlying industry distribution market capitalization, and allows investors to accurately compare equity performance across markets, regions, and sectors.

Mid-Cap U.S. Companies
Generally speaking, companies with market capitalization between $1.0 billion and $10 billion.

Nasdaq Biotechnology Index
The Nasdaq Biotechnology Index contains companies engaged in using biomedical research for the discovery or development of new treatments and cures for human disease. The index is one of eight sub-indexes of the Nasdaq Composite Index, which measures all common stocks listed on The Nasdaq Stock Market.

The Nasdaq Stock Market
The Nasdaq Stock Market, which debuted in 1971 as the world's first electronic stock market, is the fastest growing stock market in the United States. Nasdaq trades more shares per day and has a greater dollar volume of trades than any other U.S. equities market.

Post-Liquidation
Return after taxes on distributions. Assumes fund shares have not been sold.

Pre-Liquidation
Return after taxes on distributions. Assumes fund shares have not been sold.

Redeem
To exchange fund shares for their present value in either cash or "in-kind" securities.

Russell 1000 Index
This index measures the performance of the 1,000 largest companies in the Russell 3000 Index, representing approximately 92% of the total market capitalization of the Russell 3000 Index. This index also contains about 800 companies that might be considered Mid Cap with market caps between $1.0 billion and $10 billion.

Russell 2000 Index
This index measures the performance of the 2,000 smallest companies in the Russell 3000 Index, representing approximately 8% of the total market capitalization of the Russell 3000 Index. The market cap of these companies range from about $100 million to $1.2 billion.

Russell 3000 Index

This index measures the performance of 3,000 publicly held U.S. companies based on total market capitalization, which represents approximately 98% of tenantable U.S. market.

S&P 500 Index, S&P 500

Widely regarded as the standard for measuring large-cap U.S. stock market performance, this popular index includes a representative sample of leading companies in leading industries. The S&P 500 is used by 97% of U.S. money managers and pension plan sponsors. More than $750 billion is indexed to the S&P 500.

S&P MidCap 400 Index, S&P 400

Measuring the performance of the mid-size company segment of the U.S. market, this index is used by over 95% of U.S. managers and pension plan sponsors. More than $25 billion is indexed to the S&P MidCap 400.

S&P/Barra Growth and Value Indexes

Companies in each U.S. index are split into two groups based on price-to-book ratio to create growth and value indexes. The value index contains companies with lower price-to-book ratios, while the growth index contains those with higher ratios.

Small-Cap U.S. Companies

Generally speaking, companies with market capitalization less than $1.2 billion.

Tracking Error

Tracking error in terms of an active manager's return to a benchmark is often called Active Manager Risk, and expresses how much tracking error a manager of a portfolio risks while attempting to add alpha over and above an investor's benchmark. In this context, tracking error can be quantified as the standard deviation of a manager's alpha to a benchmark.

Value-Oriented Stocks

Stocks of corporations that are "cheap" by traditional yardsticks in comparison to their price/earnings ratio, price/book ratio, assets, cash flow and yield.

The World in Brief

Background:

Globally, the 20th century was marked by: (a) two devastating world wars; (b) the Great Depression of the 1930s; (c) the end of vast colonial empires; (d) rapid advances in science and technology, from the first airplane flight at Kitty Hawk, North Carolina (US) to the landing on the moon; (e) the Cold War between the Western alliance and the Warsaw Pact nations; (f) a sharp rise in living standards in North America, Europe, and Japan; (g) increased concerns about the environment, including loss of forests, shortages of energy and water, the decline in biological diversity, and air pollution; (h) the onset of the AIDS epidemic; and (i) the ultimate emergence of the US as the only world superpower. The planet's population continues to explode: from 1 billion in 1820, to 2 billion in 1930, 3 billion in 1960, 4 billion in 1974, 5 billion in 1988, and 6 billion in 2000. For the 21st century, the continued exponential growth in science and technology raises both hopes (e.g., advances in medicine) and fears (e.g., development of even more lethal weapons of war).

Geography

World

Map references:

Physical Map of the World, Political Map of the World, Standard Time Zones of the World

Area:

total: 510.072 million sq km
land: 148.94 million sq km
water: 361.132 million sq km
note: 70.8% of the world's surface is water, 29.2% is land

Area-comparative:

land area about 16 times the size of the US

Land boundaries:

the land boundaries in the world total 250,708 km (not counting shared boundaries twice); two nations, China and Russia, each border 14 other countries note: 44 nations and other areas are landlocked, these include: Afghanistan, Andorra, Armenia, Austria, Azerbaijan, Belarus, Bhutan, Bolivia, Botswana, Burkina Faso, Burundi, Central African Republic, Chad, Czech Republic, Ethiopia, Holy See (Vatican City), Hungary, Kazakhstan, Kyrgyzstan, Laos, Lesotho, Liechtenstein, Luxembourg, Macedonia, Malawi, Mali, Moldova, Mongolia, Nepal, Niger, Paraguay, Rwanda, San Marino, Serbia, Slovakia, Swaziland, Switzerland, Tajikistan, Turkmenistan, Uganda, Uzbekistan, West Bank, Zambia, Zimbabwe; two of these, Liechtenstein and Uzbekistan, are doubly landlocked

Coastline:

356,000 km

note: 98 nations and other entities are islands that border no other countries, they include: American Samoa, Anguilla, Antigua and Barbuda, Aruba, Ashmore and Cartier Islands, The Bahamas, Bahrain, Baker Island, Barbados, Bassas da India, Bermuda, Bouvet Island, British Indian Ocean Territory, British Virgin Islands, Cape Verde, Cayman Islands, Christmas Island, Clipperton Island, Cocos (Keeling) Islands, Comoros, Cook Islands, Coral Sea Islands, Cuba, Cyprus, Dominica, Europa Island, Falkland Islands (Islas Malvinas), Faroe Islands, Fiji, French Polynesia, French Southern and Antarctic Lands, Glorioso Islands, Greenland, Grenada, Guam, Guernsey, Heard Island and McDonald Islands, Howland Island, Iceland, Isle of Man, Jamaica, Jan Mayen, Japan, Jarvis Island, Jersey, Johnston Atoll, Juan de Nova Island, Kingman Reef, Kiribati, Madagascar, Maldives, Malta, Marshall Islands, Martinique, Mauritius, Mayotte, Federated States of Micronesia, Midway Islands, Montserrat, Nauru, Navassa Island, New Caledonia, New Zealand, Niue, Norfolk Island,

Northern Mariana Islands, Palau, Palmyra Atoll, Paracel Islands, Philippines, Pitcairn Islands, Puerto Rico, Reunion, Saint Helena, Saint Kitts and Nevis, Saint Lucia, Saint Pierre and Miquelon, Saint Vincent and the Grenadines, Samoa, Sao Tome and Principe, Seychelles, Singapore, Solomon Islands, South Georgia and the South Sandwich Islands, Spratly Islands, Sri Lanka, Svalbard, Tokelau, Tonga, Trinidad and Tobago, Tromelin Island, Turks and Caicos Islands, Tuvalu, Vanuatu, Virgin Islands, Wake Island, Wallis and Futuna, Taiwan

Maritime claims:

a variety of situations exist, but in general, most countries make the following claims measured from the mean low-tide baseline as described in the 1982 UN Convention on the Law of the Sea: territorial sea—12 nm, contiguous zone—24 nm, and exclusive economic zone—200 nm; additional zones provide for exploitation of continental shelf resources and an exclusive fishing zone; boundary situations with neighboring states prevent many countries from extending their fishing or economic zones to a full 200nm

Climate:

a wide equatorial band of hot and humid tropical climates—bordered north and south by subtropical temperate zones—that separate two large areas of cold and dry polar climates

Terrain:

the greatest ocean depth is the Mariana Trench at 10,924 m in the Pacific Ocean

Elevation extremes:

lowest point: Bentley Subglacial Trench—2,540 m
note: in the oceanic realm, Challenger Deep in the Mariana Trench is the lowest point, lying—10,924 m below the surface of the Pacific Ocean highest point: Mount Everest 8,850 m

Natural resources:

the rapid depletion of nonrenewable mineral resources, the depletion of forest areas and wetlands, the extinction of animal and plant species, and the deterioration in air and water quality (especially in Eastern Europe, the former USSR, and China) pose serious long-term problems that governments and peoples are only beginning to address

Land use:

arable land: 13.31%
permanent crops: 4.71%
other: 81.98% (2005)

Irrigated land:

2,770,980 sq km (2003)

Natural hazards:

large areas subject to severe weather (tropical cyclones), natural disasters (earthquakes, landslides, tsunamis, volcanic eruptions)

Environment—
current issues:

population, industrial disasters, pollution (air, water, acid rain, toxic substances), loss of vegetation (overgrazing, deforestation, desertification), loss of wildlife, soil degradation, soil depletion, erosion

Geography-note:

the world is now thought to be about 4.55 billion years old, just about one-third of the 13-billion-year age estimated for the universe

People   World
Population:

6,525,170,264 (July 2006 est.)

Age structure:

0-14 years: 27.4% (male 919,219,446/female 870,242,271)

15-64 years: 65.2% (male 2,152,066,888/female 2,100,334,722)

65 years and over: 7.4% (male 213,160,216/female 270,146,721)

note: some countries do not maintain age structure information, thus a slight discrepancy exists between the total world population and the total for world age structure (2006 est.)

Median age:

total: 27.6 years
male: 27 years
female: 28.2 years (2006 est.)

Population growth rate:

1.14% (2006 est.)

Birth rate:

20.05 births/1,000 population (2006 est.)

Death rate:

8.67 deaths/1,000 population (2006 est.)

Sex ratio:

at birth: 1.06 male(s)/female
under 15 years: 1.06 male(s)/female
15-64 years: 1.03 male(s)/female
65 years and over: 0.79 male(s)/female
total population: 1.01 male(s)/female (2006 est.)

Infant mortality rate:

total: 48.87 deaths/1,000 live births
male: 50.98 deaths/1,000 live births
female: 46.65 deaths/1,000 live births (2006 est.)

Life expectancy at birth:

total population: 64.77 years
male: 63.16 years
female: 66.47 years (2006 est.)

Total fertility rate:	2.59 children born/woman (2006 est.)
HIV/AIDS—adult prevalence rate:	NA
HIV/AIDS—people living with HIV/AIDS:	NA
HIV/AIDS—deaths:	NA
Religions:	Christians 33.03% (of which Roman Catholics 17.33%, Protestants 5.8%, Orthodox 3.42%, Anglicans 1.23%), Muslims 20.12%, Hindus 13.34%, Buddhists 5.89%, Sikhs 0.39%, Jews 0.23%, other religions 12.61%, non-religious 12.03%, atheists 2.36% (2004 est.)
Languages:	Mandarin Chinese 13.69%, Spanish 5.05%, English 4.84%, Hindi 2.82%, Portuguese 2.77%, Bengali 2.68%, Russian 2.27%, Japanese 1.99%, Standard German 1.49%, Wu Chinese 1.21% (2004 est.)
	note: percents are for "first language" speakers only
Literacy:	definition: age 15 and over can read and write
	total population: 82%
	male: 87%
	female: 77%
	note: over two-thirds of the world's 785 million illiterate adults are found in only eight countries (India, China, Bangladesh, Pakistan, Nigeria, Ethiopia, Indonesia, and Egypt); of all the illiterate adults in the world, two-thirds are women; extremely low literacy rates are concentrated in three regions, South and West Asia, Sub-Saharan Africa, and the Arab states, where around one-third of the men and half of all women are illiterate (2005 est.)

Government	*World*
Administrative divisions:	272 nations, dependent areas, and other entities
Legal system:	all members of the UN are parties to the statute that established the International Court of Justice (ICJ) or World Court

Economy	*World*
Economy— overview:	Global output rose by 4.4% in 2005, led by China (9.3%), India (7.6%), and Russia (5.9%). The other 14 successor nations of the USSR and the other old Warsaw Pact nations again experienced widely divergent growth rates; the three Baltic nations continued as strong performers, in the 7% range of growth. Growth results posted by the major industrial countries varied from no gain for Italy to a strong gain by the United States (3.5%). The developing nations also varied in their growth results, with many countries facing population increases that erode gains in output. Externally, the nation-state, as a bedrock economic-political institution, is steadily losing control over international flows of people, goods, funds, and technology. Internally, the central government often finds its control over resources slipping as separatist regional movements—typically based on ethnicity—gain momentum, e.g., in many of the successor states of the former Soviet Union, in the former Yugoslavia, in India, in Iraq, in Indonesia, and in Canada. Externally, the central government is losing decision making powers to international bodies, notably the EU. In Western Europe, governments face the difficult political problem of channeling resources away from welfare programs in order to increase investment and strengthen incentives to seek employment. The addition of 80 million people each year to an already overcrowded globe is exacerbating the problems of pollution,

desertification, underemployment, epidemics, and famine. Because of their own internal problems and priorities, the industrialized countries devote insufficient resources to deal effectively with the poorer areas of the world, which, at least from an economic point of view, are becoming further marginalized. The introduction of the euro as the common currency of much of Western Europe in January 1999, while paving the way for an integrated economic powerhouse, poses economic risks because of varying levels of income and cultural and political differences among the participating nations. The terrorist attacks on the US on 11 September 2001 accentuated a further growing risk to global prosperity, illustrated, for example, by the reallocation of resources away from investment to anti-terrorist programs. The opening of war in March 2003 between a US-led coalition and Iraq added new uncertainties to global economic prospects. After the coalition victory, the complex political difficulties and the high economic cost of establishing domestic order in Iraq became major global problems that continued into 2006.

GDP (purchasing power parity):	*GWP (gross world product): $60.63 trillion (2005 est.)*
GDP (official exchange rate):	*$43.07 trillion (2005 est.)*
GDP—real growth rate:	*4.7% (2005 est.)*
GDP—per capita (PPP):	*$9,500 (2005 est.)*
GDP—composition by sector:	*agriculture: 4%* *industry: 32%* *services: 64% (2004 est.)*
Labor force:	*3.001 billion (2005 est.)*

Labor force—by occupation:	*agriculture: 42%* *industry: 21%* *services: 37% (2002 est.)*
Unemployment rate:	*30% combined unemployment and underemployment in many non-industrialized countries; developed countries typically 4%-12% unemployment*
Household income or consumption by percentage share:	*lowest 10%: 2.6%* *highest 10%: 29.4% (2000 est.)*
Inflation rate (consumer prices):	*developed countries 1% to 4% typically; developing countries 5% to 20% typically; national inflation rates vary widely in individual cases, from declining prices in Japan to hyperinflation in one Third World countries (Zimbabwe); inflation rates have declined for most countries for the last several years, held in check by increasing international competition from several low wage countries (2005 est.)*
Industries:	*dominated by the onrush of technology, especially in computers, robotics, telecommunications, and medicines and medical equipment; most of these advances take place in OECD nations; only a small portion of non-OECD countries have succeeded in rapidly adjusting to these technological forces; the accelerated development of new industrial (and agricultural) technology is complicating already grim environmental problems*
Industrial production growth rate:	*3% (2003 est.)*

Electricity—production:	16.54 trillion kWh (2003 est.)
Electricity—consumption:	15.45 trillion kWh (2003 est.)
Electricity—exports:	537 billion kWh (2003)
Electricity—imports:	545.2 billion kWh (2003)
Oil—production:	79.65 million bbl/day (2003 est.)
Oil—consumption:	80.1 million bbl/day (2003 est.)
Oil—proved reserves:	1.349 trillion bbl (1 January 2002 est.)
Natural gas—production:	2.674 trillion cu m (2003 est.)
Natural gas—consumption:	2.675 trillion cu m (2003 est.)
Natural gas—exports:	667.6 billion cu m (2001 est.)
Natural gas—imports:	696 billion cu m (2001 est.)
Natural gas—proved reserves:	174.6 trillion cu m (1 January 2002)
Exports:	$10.33 trillion f.o.b. (2004 est.)

Exports—commodities:	the whole range of industrial and agricultural goods and services
Exports—partners:	US 15.6%, Germany 7.4%, China 5.7%, France 4.9%, UK 4.7%, Japan 4.5% (2005)
Imports:	$10.3 trillion f.o.b. (2004 est.)
Imports—commodities:	the whole range of industrial and agricultural goods and services
Imports—partners:	China 9.3%, US 9%, Germany 9%, Japan 6.1%, France 4.2% (2005)
Debt—external:	$36.89 trillion note: this figure is the sum total of all countries' external debt, both public and private (2004 est.)
Economic aid—recipient:	$154 billion official development assistance (ODA) (2004)

Communications	**World**	*Top of Page*
Telephones—main lines in use:	1,263,367,600 (2005)	
Telephones—mobile cellular:	2,168,433,600 (2005)	
Telephone system:	general assessment: NA domestic: NA international: NA	

Radio broadcast stations:	AM NA, FM NA, shortwave NA
Television broadcast stations:	NA
Internet users:	1,018,057,389 (2005)

Transportation	**World**	*Top of Page*
Airports:	49,024 (2006)	
Heliports:	2,021 (2006)	
Railways:	total: 1,115,205 km broad gauge: 257,481 km standard gauge: 671,413 km narrow gauge: 186,311 km (2003)	
Roadways:	total: 32,345,165 km paved: 19,403,061 km unpaved: 12,942,104 km (2002)	
Waterways:	671,886 km (2004)	
Merchant marine:	total: 33,222 ships (1000 GRT or over) (2006)	

Military	**World**	*Top of Page*
Military expenditures— percent of GDP:	roughly 2% of gross world product (2005 est.)	

Transnational Issues   *World*   *Top of Page*

Disputes—
international:

stretching over 250,000 km, the world's 329 international land boundaries separate the 193 independent states and 73 dependencies, areas of special sovereignty, and other miscellaneous entities; ethnicity, culture, race, religion, and language have divided states into separate political entities as much as history, physical terrain, political fiat, or conquest, resulting in sometimes arbitrary and imposed boundaries; maritime states have claimed limits and have so far established over 130 maritime boundaries and joint development zones to allocate ocean resources and to provide for national security at sea; boundary, borderland/resource, and territorial disputes vary in intensity from managed or dormant to violent or militarized; most disputes over the alignment of political boundaries are confined to short segments and are today less common and less hostile than borderland, resource, and territorial disputes; undemarcated, indefinite, porous, and unmanaged boundaries, however, encourage illegal cross-border activities, uncontrolled migration, and confrontation; territorial disputes may evolve from historical and/or cultural claims, or they may be brought on by resource competition; ethnic and cultural clashes continue to be responsible for much of the territorial fragmentation around the world; disputes over islands at sea or in rivers frequently form the source of territorial and boundary conflict; other sources of contention include access to water and mineral (especially petroleum) resources, fisheries, and arable land; nonetheless, most nations cooperate to clarify their international boundaries and to resolve territorial and resource disputes peacefully; regional discord today prevails not so much between the armed forces of independent states as between stateless armed entities that detract from the sustenance and welfare of local populations, leaving the community of nations to cope with resultant refugees, hunger, disease, impoverishment, and environmental degradation

Refugees and internally displaced persons:

the United Nations High Commissioner for Refugees (UNHCR) estimated that in December 2004 there was a global population of 9.2 million refugees, the lowest number in 25 years, and as many as 25 million IDPs in over 49 countries (2005)

Trafficking in persons:

current situation: about 600,000 to 800,000 people, mostly women and children, are trafficked annually across national borders, not including millions trafficked within their own countries; at least 80% of the victims are female; 75% of all victims are trafficked into commercial sexual exploitation; roughly two-thirds of the global victims are trafficked intra-regionally within East Asia and the Pacific (260,000 to 280,000 people) and Europe and Eurasia (170,000 to 210,000 people)

About the Author

Carl is President of the global investment advisory firm Chartwell Partners. He is a columnist on global investing with **Forbes.com** *and writes the "Global Gambits" column for* **Forbes Asia** *and is also the editor of the Chartwell ETF Global Advisor investment newsletter and the* **ChartwellETFadvisor.com** *member advisory website.*

*He is the author of "***Think Global, Grow Rich***" and the "***The New Global ETF Investor***" and, during the administration of George H.W. Bush, served on the Executive Board of Directors of the Asian Development Bank in Manila, Philippines where he led investment missions throughout Asia.*

Carl was a Vice President and opened Asia-Pacific markets for the investment bank Robert W. Baird & Company and a global ETF specialist with the Union Bank of Switzerland (UBS). He was an Asian specialist with both the U.S. Congress and the U.S. Treasury and was a member of the U.S.—Pacific Economic Cooperation Committee.

He is an economics graduate of the University of Wisconsin with a minor in Oriental Studies, received a M.A.L.D. from the Fletcher School of Law & Diplomacy, and studied Japanese at Harvard University. Carl received an economics scholarship from the U.S.-Japan Friendship Commission and studied at Sophia University and Keio University in Japan.

978-0-595-42920-2
0-595-42920-3